Great

RAILWAYS

of the World

First published 2008
Produced by AA Publishing
© Automobile Association Developments Limited 2008

Published by AA Publishing (a trading name of Automobile Association
Developments Limited, whose registered office is Fanum House, Basing View,
Basingstoke, Hampshire RG21 4EA; registered number 1878835

Visit the AA Publishing website at www.theAA.com/travel

A03798

A CIP catalogue record for this book is available from the British Library.
The contents of this book are believed correct at the time of printing.
Nevertheless, the publishers cannot be held responsible for any errors
or omissions or for changes in the details given in this book or for the
consequences of any reliance on the information it provides. This does not
affect your statutory rights. We have tried to ensure accuracy in this book, but
things do change and we would be grateful if readers would advise us of any
inaccuracies they may encounter.

Written by Julian Holland
Illustrated by Milepost 92½ – railphotolibrary.com
Senior Editor: Susan Lambert
Layout and Design: Tracey Butler
Internal Repro and Image Manipulation: Sarah Montgomery
Copy Editor: Marilynne Lanng
Proofreader: Sandy Draper
Index: Hilary Bird
Production: Lyn Kirby

Repro by MRM Graphics Ltd, Winslow
Printed by Oriental Press, Dubai

Page 3b: Locomotive No. 484 at Tanglefoot Curve, Cumbres Pass, on the Cumbres & Toltec scenic railroad in 1998.

Page 4: Norfolk & Western 'J' Class 4-8-4 No. 611 at Blue Ridge, West Virginia in 1992.

Page 6-7: Union Pacific Railroad 'Big Boy' 4-8-8-4 No. 4023 heads a freight on Sherman Hill.

Great
RAILWAYS
of the World

Julian Holland

CONTENTS

From small beginnings during Britain's Industrial Revolution in the late 18th and early 19th centuries, the railways of the world currently extend to a combined length of 1,370,782km/849,885 miles. From the opening of the first public steam railway in England, in 1825, expansion was rapid and by the early 20th century every continent of the world was crisscrossed by a network of lines built to a wide variety of different gauges. Technical development was also rapid and within 150 years, the mighty steam locomotive had been ousted by more technologically advanced diesel-electric and electric motive power. Despite competition from both road and air travel during the latter half of the 20th century, many railways of the world are now experiencing a renaissance due to environmental, economic and political issues in the 21st century. The expansion of intermodal and high-capacity bulk cargo trains, new high-speed passenger lines and commuter networks can be seen in many countries. The railways of the world have a great future!

Great Railways of the World is a celebration, both past and present, of the incredible diversity of rail transport in more than 60 countries across the globe. They include the last steam monsters of Inner Mongolia, the 'Indian Pacific' of the Australian outback, Amtrak across the magnificent Rockies and the quaint Darjeeling-Himalayan steam train in northern India, the long-lost Hejaz Railway in Saudi Arabia, the sugar-cane lines of the Philippines, the Shinkansen high-speed trains of Japan and the 'Glacier Express' in Switzerland.

Julian Holland

EUROPE

AUSTRIA

The ÖBB or Österreichische Bundesbahnen (Austrian Federal Railway) is largely electrified, receiving power through hydroelectric generation. Although electrification began as early as 1912, it wasn't until after the Second World War that wide-spread electrification took place. The last main line steam trains ceased operating in the late 1970s. The ÖBB currently operates 5,635km/3,493 miles of route and employs more than 40,000 people, making it one of the largest employers in Austria.

▲ *The ÖBB currently operates around 1,200 locomotives of which around 900 are electric powered. Locomotives, such as this old Class 1141 Bo-Bo locomotive, have been replaced by more modern and powerful classes such as the 1016, 1116 and 1216 which operate on dual voltages to enable them to haul international trains to neighbouring countries.*

▶ *Seen here amidst glorious Alpine scenery at the ski resort of St Jakob in 1999, the Austrian Federal Railways Class 1044 Bo-Bo electric locomotives were introduced between 1974 and 1995. Weighing 84 tonnes each and with a power output of 6,900hp, over 200 of these powerful locomotives were built by Simmering-Graz-Pauker in Graz.*

▶ Also known as the Krimml branch, the Pinzgauer Lokalbahn is a 760mm/2ft 6in narrow gauge line that runs in the valley of the River Salzach between Zell am See and Krimml, at a height of nearly 400m/1,312ft, the site of Europe's highest waterfall. Opened in 1898, the 53km/33-mile line is operated by Austrian Federal Railways (OBB). Following damage to the trackbed caused by flooding in 2005, services were cut back to Mittershill but OBB plan to reopen the entire line to Krimml by the end of 2009. Passenger services are normally diesel-hauled apart from the summer months when steam locomotives such as No. 399.01, seen here at Zell am See, also operate tourist trains.

▼ Steam traction operated on the Iron Mountain Railway in Styria until 1978, when the heavily laden trains carrying iron-ore from the mines at Erzberg to the foundries at Eisenerz and Vordernberg were normally headed and banked by these powerful 0-6-2 tank locomotives. Following electrification of the line in 1978 the rack system was taken out of use, but within ten years the ore traffic had ceased and the line had closed. However, since 1990, part of the line has been reopened as a tourist railway and is now operated by the Erzbergbahn Society.

AZORES

Far out in the Atlantic Ocean the Portuguese islands of the Azores are a strange place to find decaying relics of Isambard Kingdom Brunel's unique broad gauge.

▲ ▶ *To assist with the construction of a new harbour at Ponto Delgado, a 2,140mm/7ft gauge railway was built on the island of San Miguel in the 1860s. Two broad gauge steam locomotives were ordered from England to haul stone bearing trains from quarries to the site of a new breakwater. Although construction work was completed by 1888, the railway was brought back to life after the Second World War to assist with road construction on the island and again in the late 1960s during construction of a pier. The only surviving examples of broad gauge locomotives in the world, they now languish in a Port Authority shed awaiting possible restoration. They are seen here in a dilapidated condition, in 1981, on a short length of 2,140mm/7ft gauge track at Ponto Delgado – (above) an 0-4-0 saddle tank built by Falcon Works of Loughborough (right), another 0-4-0 saddle tank, this one built by Black Hawthorn of Gateshead.*

BELGIUM

The first railway in Belgium, from Brussels to Mechelen, opened in 1835. Operated by the SNCB (Société Nationale des Chemins de Fer Belges) since 1926, the current network length is 3,415km/2,117 miles of which 2,512km/1,557 miles are electrified. Hauled by Type 29 locomotive 29.013, the last regular main line steam train in Belgium ran from Aat to Denderleeuw on 20 December 1966. This locomotive, built after the Second World War by Canada's Montréal Locomotive Works, has since been preserved.

▲ In 1999, overlooked by the gleaming train shed of Antwerp station, SNCB Class 27 Bo-Bo electric locomotive No. 2713 waits to depart. Developing 5,650hp each, a total of 60 Class 27 electric locomotives were delivered to SNCB between 1981 and 1984. These powerful, versatile locomotives haul both express passenger and heavy freight trains.

▶ Introduced in 1988, a total of 52 of these Class AM86 electric multiple units are operated by SNCB on commuter and local services in and around Brussels, Antwerp and Liège. Here, a member of this class stands at Brussels Midi station in July 1996.

CROATIA

Following the breakup of former Yugoslavia, modernisation of Croatia's railways has proceeded at a slow pace. Currently only about a third of the current network is electrified and many of the main routes are still single track. Following the pattern set in many other European countries, tilting trains have been introduced, initially on the lucrative Zagreb to Split route. Croatian Railways (Hrvatske zeljeznice/HZ) also operates international services to Slovenia, Hungary, Bosnia and Herzegovina, and Serbia.

▲ *Designed for short distance local passenger transport, ten of these rather quaint Class 7221 diesel railcars together with unpowered trailer cars, were built by Uerdingen of Brunswick, Germany, 1955, with a further batch built under licence in Yugoslavia in 1969. Numbers of this class have dwindled as they have been replaced by more modern diesel multiple units. Here, a member of this class – nicknamed 'Schienenbus' – is seen on duty at Karlovac station in May 2001.*

▶ *The main railway trunk route in Croatia is the line between Dobova, on the border with Slovenia, and Tovarrik, on the border with Serbia. Unlike many others in Croatia it is a fairly modern, double-track electrified line and passes through the capital city, Zagreb. Here a Class 6111 electric multiple unit waits at Glavni Kolodvor station, Zagreb in May 2001.*

CZECH REPUBLIC

Since the breakup of Czechoslovakia in 1993, the majority of railways in the Czech Republic have been operated by Ceské dráhy (Czech Republic Railways/CD). With around 60,000 employees the company is the biggest employer in the country and the fifth-largest freight operator in Europe. Out of a total route length of 9,492km/5,885 miles, only 3,071km/1,904 miles are currently electrified.

▲ *Introduced in 1980, a total of 181 of these dual-voltage Class 363 electric locomotives were built by Skoda in former Czechoslovakia. Following the split of the country into two separate states, members of this class were shared between the CD (Czech Republic Railways) and ZSSK (Slovakian Railways). Here a member of this class is seen on a passenger train at Brno in October 2005.*

▶ *The former Czechoslovakia had a long tradition of building beautifully designed and powerful steam locomotives. Long after the end of steam in most parts of Western Europe, many remained in regular service until the late 1970s. Popular on local passenger trains, this Class 354, 4-6-2 tank locomotive was developed from the Austrian 629 Class. Around 40 former Czechoslovakian steam locomotives are preserved in working order in the Czech Republic and Slovakia.*

DENMARK

The first steam railway in Denmark opened between Copenhagen and Roskilde in 1847. Founded in 1885, Danish State Railways (Danske Statsbahner/DSB) was the principal rail operator in the country until the late 20th century when parts of it, such as goods transport, were privatised. Until the opening of the Little Belt Bridge in 1935, and the great Belt Fixed Link in 1987, railways in the three separate parts of Denmark were linked by train ferries. DSB currently operates 2,644km/1,642 miles of standard gauge lines in Denmark of which a total of 636km/395 miles are electrified.

▲ ▶ *Electrification of Denmark's main railway system came much later than in other Western European countries. The first line to be electrified was between Copenhagen and Elsinore in 1986 and this was followed in the 1990s by the main line across Zealand to South Jutland. Currently only 446km/277 miles out of a total of 2,644km/1,642 route miles has been electrified and consequently many local passenger services are still operated by diesel multiple units such as the Class MR sets which were introduced more than 30 years ago. Members of this rather outdated class are seen here at Tinglev (above) on the South Jutland peninsula in 1997 and at Arhar (right) in 1999.*

ESTONIA

Railways in the former Soviet republic of Estonia were built to a gauge of 1,520mm/4ft 11⅞in. Of the 991km/614 miles of track only 132km/82 miles are electrified. In recent years, the main rail operator, EVR (Eesti Raudtee), has suffered a large drop in freight traffic due to increased competition from road hauliers.

▲ *Seen here in 2002, this is the only existing example of the Class MEV-1 electric motor car, which was introduced in 1974. This unusual vehicle was rebuilt from a Class ER2 and is now operated by Elektriraudtee and used for shunting on the electrified lines around Tallinn.*

▶ *A total of 56 of these Class C36-71 Co-Co diesels were bought secondhand by EVR (Eesti Raudtee) in 2002 from Union Pacific in the US. Designed to haul heavy freight trains, such as this eastbound one seen at Tapa in July 2002, these locomotives were originally built by General Electric as Class 1500 in 1985. However, since this photograph was taken, freight traffic on the EVR has seen a huge drop.*

FINLAND

Until independence in 1917, Finland was a Grand Principality of Russia. Consequently, the railways in Finland were built to the wider Russian gauge of 1,524mm/5ft. The first railway between Helsinki and Hämeenlinna was opened in 1862 and by 1950 most Finnish broad gauge railways had been incorporated into the Finnish State Railways system. Electrification of much of the main line network started in the 1960s and steam had vanished by the mid 1970s. Until its withdrawal in 1974, the 22 members of the Class Hr1 4-6-2 locomotives were the last Pacific steam locomotives in regular use in Western Europe.

▲ *A short time before the end of regular steam haulage in Finland this Class Vr3 0-10-0 tank spent its time shunting at Seinäjoki on 24 March 1972. Weighing 78 tonnes these powerful tank locomotives were introduced in the 1920s.*

▶ *Totalling 148 members, the Class Tv1 (or 'Jumbos' as they were known) 2-8-0 locomotives were introduced in 1917 and continued in service on main line duties until 1974. Here, one of this class makes an impressive sight as it struggles out of the sand quarries at Hyrynsalmi with a loaded train in March 1972.*

FRANCE

The first railway in France, between Lyon and St Etienne, opened in 1831. Today, thanks to government foresight and vast investment, the railways of France are among the most modern in the world. The main rail operator, SNCF (Société Nationale des Chemins de Fer Français) currently has a network of 29,046km/18,009 miles, of which more than 15,000km/9,300 miles are electrified.

▲ *Introduced in 1926, the 'Fleche d'Or' was a luxury train that ran between Paris Gare du Nord and Calais, where passengers took a ferry to Dover to join the 'Golden Arrow' that carried them in Pullman cars to London's Victoria Station. Seen here hauled by a Class 231K 4-6-2 at Pont du Bergues near Dunkirk in 1968, this famous train made its last run on 30 September 1972. The SNCF Class 231 locomotives were first introduced in 1909 by the Paris-Lyon-Mediterranee (PLM) and over the ensuing years were constantly improved with many different variations of which the final version was the 231 K. Several members of this class have been preserved and one, the 231 K 82, starred in the 1974 film 'Borsalino' with Alain Delon.*

▶ *The SNCF TGV (Train à Grandes Vitesse) Sud-Est electric multiple units were built by Alstom and operated the first high-speed TGV service from Paris to Lyon in 1981. A total of 107 sets were built between 1978 and 1988 and each set comprises two power cars and eight carriages with seating for 345 passengers. These trains operate at speeds of up to 300km/h (186mph) and are found in service between Paris and Lyon and on the newer LGV (Lignes à Grande Vitesse) Méditerranée to Lyon. The original orange livery, as seen in this photograph, has been replaced by the silver-and-blue livery of the TGV Atlantique.*

◀ Thalys is a train-operating company that runs high-speed services between Paris, Brussels and Amsterdam. Based on the SNCF TGV Réseau electric multiple units built by Alstom between 1992 and 1996, the ten TGV Thalys PBA sets are equipped to operate on the different electrical systems of each of the three countries that they serve at speeds of up to 300km/h (186mph).

▼ Introduced in 1913, the 141 TB Class of powerful 2-8-2 tank locomotives ended their days hauling suburban trains from the Gare de Bastille in Paris. Here, two members of the class are seen resting in the Nogent-Vincennes roundhouse in 1968, one year before the end of steam on this line. Two members of this class have since been preserved.

▲ Following on from the success of the TGV Sud-Est high-speed electric multiple units, 105 units of the TGV Atlantique were built by Alstom for SNCF between 1988 and 1991. Capable of operating on two different electrical systems, these units were introduced into service on the newly opened LGV Atlantique from Paris to western France in 1989. Each unit is made up of two power cars and ten carriages with seating for 485 passengers. Specially modified TGV Atlantique Unit No. 325 set a new world rail-speed record of 515km/h (320mph) on 18 May 1990. The world rail-speed record is currently held by TGV 4402 which achieved 574km/h (356mph) on the newly constructed LGV Est on 3 April 2007.

◄ A total of 370 of these powerful Class 140 C 2-8-0 mixed-traffic locomotives were built between 1913 and 1917 for the Chemin de Fer de l'Etat. After the outbreak of the First World War, the final 200 locomotives of this class were built by Nasmyth, Wilson of Manchester and the North British Locomotive Company of Glasgow. By the early 1970s the remaining members of this class became the last steam locomotives still in regular use on SNCF. Eight members of this prolific class have since been preserved. A Class 140 C is seen here posing on the turntable in Verdun roundhouse in 1968.

▶ Operating high-speed services through the Channel Tunnel between London, Paris and Brussels, Eurostar trains are classified as Class 373 in the UK and TGV-TMST (TransManche Super Train) in France. Capable of normal operating speeds of up to 300km/h (186mph), a total of 38 trainsets were built by GEC-Alsthom between 1992 and 1996 of which 31 sets consist of two power cars and 18 carriages with seating for 750 passengers, while seven shorter sets consist of two power cars and 14 carriages, with seating for 558 passengers. A Eurostar train currently holds the UK rail-speed record of 334km/h (207mph), which was achieved on the new Channel Tunnel Rail Link near the Nashenden Valley in Kent on 30 July 2003.

GERMANY

The first steam railway in Germany, from Nürnberg to Fürth, opened in 1835. Although Germany was reunified in 1990, it wasn't until 1994 that the two separate rail systems of East Germany (Deutsche Reichsbahn) and West Germany (Deutsche Bundesbahn) were unified. Today, with a massive network of 35,540km/22,035 miles, of which 19,335km/11,988 miles is electrified, DB AG (Deutsche Bahn AG, or Die Bahn as it is now known) is the German national rail company with more than 200,000 employees.

▲ *Known as the V-160 family of diesel locomotives and the workhorse of DB (Deutsche Bundesbahn) for many years, the Class 218 is a development of the original Class 216 of which more than 200 units were built between 1960 and 1969. A total of 410 units of the more powerful Class 218 were built for DB between 1971 and 1979. Despite their age, some modified members of this class are still employed on freight trains. Resplendent in its orange livery, a member of this handsome class is seen here at the head of a passenger train at Cologne in 1986.*

▶ *Opened in 1930, the Bayerische Zugspitzbahn is a metre-gauge electric rack-and-pinion railway that runs from Garmisch-Partenkirchen to the summit of the Zugspitze. Located in the Bavarian Alps close to the German-Austrian border, the Zugspitze (2,963 m/9,721 ft) is the highest peak in Germany and is home to a meteorological observatory.*

Bayerische Zugspitzbahn

▶ *Introduced in 1974, the DB Class 181 Bo-Bo electric locomotives were fitted with dual-voltage controls to enable them to operate trains to France and Luxembourg. Now being replaced by more modern locos, only a handful of the original 25 that were built are still in operation. Pictured here is a member of this class threading its way through the network of points as it arrives at Frankfurt in 2001.*

▼ *Opened in 1895, the 600mm/1ft 11⅝in narrow gauge Muskau Forest Railway served small factories, coal mines and the forestry industry near the health resort of Bad Muskau in Saxony. Originally horse-drawn, redundant steam locomotives from the German Military Railways were introduced after the First World War. The little line was kept busy until the 1970s transporting coal to local factories, clay to brickworks and roof tile factories, and mud to a health spa treatment bath. The line closed in 1978 but since 1995 has been reopened as a tourist line. Motive power is provided by ex-brickworks diesel locomotives and a 0-8-0 tank of 1918 vintage. Here a former First World War locomotive is seen in operation on the line in 1977, a year before closure.*

▲ A coal-fired Deutsche Bundesbahn (DB) Class 44 2-10-0 makes a fine sight as it heads a heavy freight between Koblenz and Trier on the busy Mosel Valley line near Cochem in 1970. Along with over 7,000 Class 52 Kriegslokomotiven (war locomotives), the numerous and powerful Class 44 locomotives were the mainstay of heavy German freight trains during the Second World War and up to the end of mainline steam in former West Germany in the 1970s.

▲ In the heart of Germany's wine-growing area, two German Class 44 2-10-0s cross the Mosel River with a heavy freight in 1969. Introduced in 1926, a total of 1,753 locomotives of this standard 3-cylinder freight class were built by 1944. Many were converted to oil firing by both the Deutsche Reichsbahn (East Germany) and Deutsche Bundesbahn (West Germany) after the Second World War.

▲ Introduced in 1925, 231 members of the Class 01 4-6-2 passenger locomotives had been built for the Deutsche Reichsbahn-Gesellschaft by 1935. Many of these fine 2-cylinder locomotives were rebuilt by the Deutsche Reichsbahn (East Germany) after the Second World War and remained in regular main line use until the late 1970s. Here, a member of this class is seen hauling a Berlin to Dresden express in 1977.

▲ Seen here in Frankfurt in 2001, the DB Class 411 high-speed electric multiple units were introduced in 1999. Known as ICE-T, a total of 62 seven-car units with tilting technology were built to operate high-speed passenger services on existing main lines in Germany. Members of this class now also operate international expresses to Switzerland and Austria. Three similar units were built for ÖBB (Austrian State Railways) in 2007.

GREECE

The first railway in Greece, between Athens and Piraeus, opened in 1869. Today there is a total of 1,435km/890 miles of standard gauge track, of which 764km/474 miles is electrified, and 983km/609 miles of narrow gauge track are still in operation.

▲ Following the end of steam on Greek railways many locomotives ended up in this graveyard in Thessaloniki in the east of the country. Here an Austrian Empire-designed Greek LA Class 2-10-0 lies abandoned in 1979. Today, Thessaloniki – the second largest city in Greece – is a major railway junction with international trains running to most of the Balkan countries.

▶ Towards the end of steam haulage on Greek railways in 1972, this former USATC oil-burning Class S160 belches columns of black smoke as it heads south on the main line to Athens. A total of 2,120 of these 2-8-0 heavy freight locomotives were built in the US for the United States Army Transportation Corps for use in Europe during the Second World War. After the war they worked on railways across the world, including most European countries as well as in Africa, Asia and South America. Greece received 27 members of this class in 1947 and purchased a further 25 from Italy in 1959.

HUNGARY

The first steam railway in Hungary, running between Pest and Vác, opened in 1846. Today the main railway operator, Magyar Államvasutak (MÁV), runs a network of 7,183km/4,453 miles, of which 2,628km/1,629 miles is electrified. In response to escalating losses many of Hungary's rural railways were closed in 2007.

▲ Still using locomotives built in the 1960s and 1970s, the Hungarian diesel locomotive fleet is now fairly ancient. Introduced in 1972, the MAV Class M41 B-B diesels are one of the workhorses of Hungarian State Railways (Magyar Allamvasutak or MAV). A total of 114 of these machines were built, of which 70 are fitted with electrical train heating and have been reclassified as Class 2241. The rest have been reclassified as Class 2341 and are based at Szombathely and Miskolc. Here a member of this class is seen hauling a passenger train near the town of Csorna in northwest Hungary in August 2003.

▶ Built by Bombardier/ELIN, the Class 5342 Talent electric multiple units were introduced in 2006 and are designed to operate on dual voltage systems for services to Austria and Slovakia. Here, a Class 5342 set is seen at Budapest Déli station (also known as Southern Railway Station) in July 2007.

▶ Steam locomotive manufacturing ceased in Hungary in 1958. Despite the wholesale introduction of both diesel and electric traction and more recent mass closures of rural lines, steam still lingered on in a few industrial locations until the 1990s. Here a former MAV Class 318 tank engine is seen working alongside an older industrial locomotive at a steelworks in 1990. At least a dozen Hungarian steam locomotives have been preserved in working order, ranging from an 1870-built Class III No. 269 to two 1955-built Class 424 2-8-0s, Nos. 424.247 and 424.287.

IRELAND

Ireland's first railway was the Dublin & Kingstown railway which opened in 1834. Strangely, the mainline track gauge of 1,600mm/5ft 3in that was adopted was different to that chosen for the rest of the British Isles and western Europe standard gauge of 1,435mm/4ft 8½in. Many narrow gauge railways were also built in Ireland to a gauge of 3ft. Route mileage had reached a peak of over 3,000 miles by 1920 but since then mass closures, including all of the narrow gauge lines, have reduced this to less than half of that amount. Due to the lack of local sources of coal, steam haulage was ousted by dieselisation in the late-1950s – much earlier than in many other European countries.

▲ *Since the mid-1960s all diesel-electric locomotives supplied for use on the main line railways in Ireland have been built by General Motors Electro-Motive Division from assembly lines in both the US and Canada. With a power output of 2,250hp, 18 members of the Class 071 Co-Co locos were delivered to CIÉ (Córas Iompair Éireann) in the late 1970s. Three similar machines were also delivered to Northern Ireland Railways in the early 1980s for use on Belfast to Dublin expresses. Here, a Class 071 heads along the scenic coast at Bray Head with a Dublin to Rosslare express in 2004. Formerly part of the Dublin and South Eastern Railway, the stretch of line between Bray and Wicklow had to be rebuilt further inland here due to coastal erosion – clearly illustrated by the disused tunnel mouth on the right.*

▶ *This is the ultimate modern train, but harking back to the days when the railways carried all commodities. Here, the past, in the shape of an old semaphore signal, contrasts vividly with a modern diesel-electric locomotive as it trundles through beautiful Irish countryside hauling a train of empty beer barrels in 2003.*

▲ Headed by a General Motors Class 071 locomotive, a Dublin to Rosslare express crosses the marshes near Rosslare in 2004. Currently three trains each day connect Rosslare Europort (for ferry routes to the UK), with Dublin Connolly station, along one of Ireland's most scenic rail routes. The train is made up of six British Rail InterCity coaches, fitted with bogies re-gauged to 1,600mm/5ft 3in, and a generator van which supplies power for the air-conditioning system.

◀ A General Motors Class 071 diesel-electric locomotive passes from single-line working to enter the passing loop at Rathdrum station on the Dublin to Rosslare line in 2004. Originally opened in 1863, Rathdrum is served by up to six trains a day to and from Dublin Connolly station. The antiquated lower-quadrant signalling on this line has now been replaced by colour-light signalling controlled from Dublin.

▶ The Dublin Area Rapid Transit system, or DART, was a major leap forward in Irish railway development when it opened in 1984. Powered by 1500V DC collected from overhead wires, the DART system provides an excellent suburban service for commuters into Dublin. Services run fron Malahide and Howth, north of Dublin, to Greystones on the coast in Co. Wicklow, via Dublin Connolly station. Plans are also now at an advanced stage to extend the DART system to the west of Dublin.

ITALY

The first steam railway in Italy, between Napoli and Portici, opened in 1839. Today the main railway operator, Ferrovie dello Stato (FS), operates a 16,295km/10,103-mile network, of which 10,688km/6,627 miles is electrified. There are also numerous other railway companies that operate both standard gauge and narrow gauge lines on the mainland and also on the islands of Sardinia and Sicily.

▲ *Railways in mountainous countries are now normally powered by electricity generated through hydroelectric power. In 1902, Italy became the first country in the world to introduce electric traction on an entire railway route with the electrification of the mountainous Valtellina line in the north of the country. Here a modern FS Class Y69 heads a push-pull train in wintry conditions at San Candido near the Austrian border in 2005.*

▶ *Tilting trains allow passenger trains to run on existing railway tracks at higher speeds than would normally be allowed. Following experiments in many countries with this form of technology the most successful to date has been the 'Italian Pendolino' train. The first of this type, the ETR 401, was introduced in 1975 on Italian State Railways. Following extensive trials a fleet of these tilting trains, known as Class ETR 450 and seen here under construction at the Fiat plant in 1986, was introduced in the 1980s. Later models of these Pendolino trains have been exported to other European countries, including the UK, where they are now used by Virgin Trains on the West Coast Main Line.*

LUXEMBOURG

Sandwiched between Belgium, France and Germany, The Grand Duchy of Luxembourg is one of the smallest countries in the world. Opened in 1859, the first railway in Luxembourg linked Luxembourg City with Thionville in France. Today, this little country operates an impressive 267km/165 miles of standard gauge railway line, the majority of it electrified.

▲ *Seen here in October 1990, the CFL (Chemins de Fer Luxembourgeois) Class 3600 Bo-Bo electric locomotives were introduced in 1958 and hauled their last regular train in March 2005. All 20 members of this class are now withdrawn but two examples have been saved for preservation. Their duties have been taken over by the more modern Class 4000 electric locomotives.*

▶ *To replace its ageing fleet of Class 3600 electric locomotives, CFL ordered 20 Class 4000 Bo-Bo locos from Bombardier, the giant Canadian company, in 2004. With its acquisition of companies such as the German-Swedish company of ADtranz in 2001, Bombardier is now the largest manufacturer of railway rolling stock in the world. Here a new Class 4000 and double-decker rolling stock wait to depart from Luxembourg City station with a local train for Troisvierges in 2008.*

NETHERLANDS

The first steam railway in the Netherlands, between Amsterdam and Haarlem, opened in 1839.
Employing more than 27,000 people, the main railway operator today, Nederlandse Spoorwegen (NS),
operates a network of 2,776km/1,721 miles, of which 2,028km/1,257 miles is electrified. The Dutch rail
network is reckoned to be one of the busiest in the world.

▲ *Founded in 2000, Railion is a major European railway cargo company made up of former national freight carrying companies in Germany, the Netherlands,
Denmark, Italy and Switzerland. The company, with its headquarters in Mainz in Germany, currently employs around 25,000 people and owns and operates
more than 2,700 locomotives and nearly 100,000 freight wagons. Here, a Railion tanker train speeds through Echt, a city in the Dutch province of Limburg,
in October 2005.*

▶ *Despite electrification of much of the NS (Nederlandse Spoorwegen) network these old style semaphore signals were still in use at Maastricht in 1985. The city
of Maastricht in the southeast of the Netherlands has two railway stations, Maastricht Central and Maastricht Randwyck. An important railway junction, Maastricht
is served by trains to Liège in Belgium and to Alkamaar with connections to Eindhoven, Utrecht and Amsterdam.*

POLAND

The first steam railway in Poland runs between Warsaw and Kraków and opened in 1835. Polish State Railways only came into being following the country's independence in 1918. Employing around 125,000 people, the main railway operator (split into many subsidiary companies since 2001) is Polskie Koleje Panstwowe (PKP) which operates a 19,435km/12,050-mile network, of which 11,953km/7,411 miles is electrified. A further 394km/244 miles of the old Russian 'broad' gauge track is operated by PKP for international services to the Ukraine.

▲ Introduced in 1971, nearly 1,200 of these Class ET22 Co-Co electric locomotives were built for the PKP (Polskie Koleje Panstwowe) to haul heavy freight and passenger trains. Despite many of this class being withdrawn, nearly 600 still remain in service. Here, characterised by its three enormous headlights, a member of this prolific class is seen hauling a coal train in 2006.

▶ A development of the Class Pt31 2-8-2 built before the Second World War, 180 of PKP Class Pt47 2-8-2 steam locomotives were built at the Fablok and Cegielski factories in Poland between 1948 and 1951. Here seen heading a cross-country train near Byden in 1983, several members of this class have since been preserved.

▲ Located in northeast Poland, only 32km/20 miles from the border with Belarus, is the town of Czarna Bialostocka. A heavily forested area, it was here that one of the last 600mm/1ft 11⅝in gauge Feldbahns, or Field Railway, was still operating in 1983. Seen here, fitted with a rickety spark-arresting chimney, an ancient steam locomotive from the former German trench railways of the First World War struggles through the forest with its load of timber.

◄ The area around Wolsztyn in western Poland is among the last places in the world where regular steam-hauled mainline trains are still operated. In 2007 there were two steam-hauled passenger trains a day from Wolsztyn to the city of Poznan, plus other services to Lezno and Zbaszynek. Freight trains in the area are also steam hauled. Steam locomotives still operating from Wolsztyn motive-power depot include examples of PKP Class Ol 49 2-6-2, Class Pt 47 2-8-2, Class Pm 36 4-6-2 and Class Ty 2-10-0. Here, PKP Class Ol 49 No. 69 is seen hauling a Poznan to Wolsztyn train at Grodzisk in April 2002.

PORTUGAL

The first railway in Portugal opened in 1856 between Lisbon and Carregado. A track gauge of 1,676mm/ 5ft 6in was adopted following the example set by railways in neighbouring Spain. This unusually wide gauge has since made direct rail connection with the rest of Europe difficult. Currently there are 2,512km/1,560 miles of broad gauge and only 175km/109 miles of narrow gauge lines operating in the country.

▲ *The Sabor Line was one of many metre-gauge (3ft 3⅜ in) railways that connected with the Portuguese State Railways main line in the Douro Valley. The line used small railcars and the unusual 2-4-6-0 Mallet compound tank engines dating from 1911. Here, No. E204, one of these Mallet locomotives, heads a mixed train from Duas Igrejas to Pocinho, north of Carvicais on 7 May 1977.*

▶ *Portugal once had hundreds of kilometres of metre-gauge (3ft 3⅜in) railway lines with most of the network in the wine-growing area in the north of the country. The busiest network was based at Porto's Trindade station from where trains ran to Senhora da Hora, Povoa de Varzim and Fafe, To the east of Porto lies the Douro Valley and here there were four completely separate metre-gauge lines serving the wine-growing tributary valleys of the Douro. Motive power was provided by a variety of steam locomotives including the powerful 0-4-4-0 Mallet tanks built by Henschel in 1905. One of these locomotives can be seen here at Porto Trindade station in 1970. Although many of these lines have since closed, a few of the Douro tributary valley lines still cling to life with diesel railcars providing a passenger service.*

ROMANIA

The first public railway in Romania opened between Oravita and Buzias in 1854. Today, with more than 20,930km/13,000 miles of track – of which nearly 40 per cent is electrified – Romanian State Railways (CFR) operates the fourth-largest rail system in Europe. Direct rail links to Ukraine, Moldova, Hungary, Serbia and Bulgaria generate additional international traffic.

▲ *Built by Siemens AG in 2003, a modern Class 96 Desiro diesel multiple unit passes underneath electric catenaries near Predeal in July 2007. Popular with tourists and walkers, Predeal is a mountain resort in central Romania.*

▶ *Most of Romania's electric locomotives were built by two national companies, Electroputere Craiova and Koncar Zagreb. CFR currently operates more than 1,000 electric locomotives, the majority of which were built by Electroputere, such as this Class 41 Co-Co seen at the head of a passenger train at Predeal in July 2007. Note the curious combination of single- and double-deck coaches employed on this train, which is classified as Accelerat by CFR.*

RUSSIA

The first steam railway in Russia, between St Petersburg and Tsarskoye Selo, opened in 1837. From 1842, all Russian 'standard' gauge railways were built to a gauge of 1,524mm/5ft – slightly wider than the gauge of 1,435mm/4ft 8½in adopted in most of Western Europe and North America. Employing 1.2 million people, the main railway operator today, Rossiyskye Zheleznye Dorogi (RZD), operates a 85,500km/53,010 miles of network, of which 40,800km/25,296 miles is electrified. This vast railway empire, stretching from the Polish border in the west to Vladivostock in the east, transported 1,311 billion tonnes of freight in 2006.

▲ ▶ The last steam locomotive was built in the USSR in 1956 and by the 1960s steam power to the west of the Urals had been replaced by diesel and electric locomotives. However, to the east of the Urals in the vast wastes of Siberia, the picture was very different. Although steam power officially ended in 1973, it is now known that steam continued to be used well into the late 1980s and that a special reserve of 1,000 steam locomotives was kept serviceable in case of a national emergency. It is also reliably reported that steam power was even used in the late 1990s to haul long-distance passenger trains on the Trans-Siberian Railway. A strategic reserve of several hundred steam locomotives is still held on the vast Krasnoyarsk Railway, the major railway operating company in Eastern Siberia. Obviously not included as part of this reserve, this former Russian Railways 2-10-0 (right) was found abandoned in 1990 at Manzhouli, a railway town that straddles the Russia–China border in Inner Mongolia. However, this powerful Trans-Siberian Class P36 4-8-4 (above), one of 250 built between 1950 and 1956, looks very much alive as it is overtaken by a long, electrically-hauled freight train in 1992.

SLOVAKIA

The first steam railway in Slovakia (then part of Hungary), to Vienna, opened in 1848. Following the breakup of former Czechoslovakia in 1993, railways in Slovakia have been operated by Zeleznice Slovenskej Republiky (ZSR). Since 2005 ZSR has been responsible only for the infrastructure – 3,509km/2,176 miles of standard gauge line plus short lengths of narrow gauge and 'Russian' broad gauge – with ZSSK operating passenger services and ZSCS operating freight services.

▲ *With its distinctive orange-and-yellow livery and its dated Soviet-bloc design, this ZSR (Zeleznice Slovenskej Republiky) Class 240 Bo-Bo electric locomotive makes a fine sight as it heads a freight train at Bratislava. Built by Skoda as Class S499.0, 145 locomotives of this class were introduced in 1968 for use on local passenger services in former Czechoslovakia. The capital of Slovakia, Bratislava is an important railway hub with direct international connections to Austria, Hungary and the Czech Republic.*

▶ *Similar in design to the ZSR Class 240 this CD (Ceske Drahy) Class 230 – here seen on an eastbound cross-border freight train at Bratislava in February 2005 – was built by Skoda in 1966 as Class S489.0 of the former Czechoslovakian State Railways. A total of 82 of these powerful Bo-Bo electric freight locomotives were built by Skoda.*

SLOVENIA

As part of a railway line from Vienna to Trieste, the first steam railway in Slovenia (then part of the Austrian Empire) opened in 1844. Today, Slovenske Zeleznice (SZ), created in 1991 after the break-up of Yugoslavia, operates a network of 1,228km/761 miles, of which 503km/312 miles is electrified.

▲ *Showing its distinctly French origins, this SZ (Slovenske Zeleznice) Class 363 C-C electric locomotive No.033 stands with an Austrian-bound freight at Ljubljana in September 2005. Originally built by Alsthom in France, 39 of these powerful locomotives, codenamed Brigitte, were delivered to the former Yugoslavian State Railways in the mid-1970s.*

▶ *Located close to the Austrian border and overlooked by the Karavanke Mountains, this SZ multiple unit trundles up the Upper Sava Valley near the town of Jesenice in August 2003. The first railway came to Jesenice in 1870, followed by the heavily engineered Karavanke Bohinj railway which was inaugurated in the early 20th century by Archduke Franz Ferdinand of Austria. The latter line opened rail connection to Austria and Italy and greatly assisted the development of the local steelworks which still operates in Jesenice today.*

SPAIN

Not only was Spain rather slow in building railways compared to other Western European countries – the first steam railway opened from Barcelona in 1848 – but the gauge chosen as standard in Spain was 1,674mm/ 5ft 6in – much wider than other European countries. Formed in 1941, the main rail operator Red Nacional de los Ferrocarriles Españoles (RENFE) currently operates a network of 11,757km/7,289 miles of broad gauge lines, of which 6,424km/3,983 miles are electrified. New high-speed electrified lines are currently being built to the European standard gauge of 1,435mm/4ft 8.5in to enable through-running of trains to and from France. Several separate companies operate a network of metre-gauge (3ft 3⅜in) lines in northern Spain.

▲ *Worked since Roman times, the Rio Tinto copper mines in southwestern Spain are among the most important in the world and by the early 20th century many hundreds of these mines had been linked by a network of narrow gauge railway lines. Seen here in forlorn retirement on the Rio Tinto system in 1987 is this 0-6-0 tank built by Dübs of Glasgow.*

▶ *The Sabero opencast colliery was located at the end of a short branch line from Cistierna on the La Robla Railway between Bilbao and Leon in northern Spain. By the late 1980s this 600mm/1ft 11⅝in gauge colliery railway had become one of the last Spanish industrial railways to operate steam locomotives. Here, 0-6-0 tank El Esla, built by Sharp Stewart of Manchester in the 1880s, is seen hard at work on this delightful industrial narrow gauge system in 1987.*

SWEDEN

The first steam railway in Sweden, between Örebro and Nora, opened in 1856. Today, Sweden's railways are operated by numerous companies, of which Statens Järnvägar (SJ AB) is the largest. The infrastructure is managed by one company, Banverket (BV) which is responsible for the maintenance of 9,782km/6,065 miles of standard gauge line, of which 7,190km/4,458 miles is electrified.

▲ *Built by Bombardier and introduced in 2002, a powerful LKAB 360-tonne double Co-Co + Co-Co electric locomotive hauls a heavy iron ore train through Nattavaara in northern Sweden in 2002. Operated by state-owned Luossavaara-Kiirunavaara Aktiebolag (LKAB), the largest underground iron ore mines in the world are located at Kiruna in northern Sweden. The mined iron ore is transported by rail to either the port of Lulea on the Gulf of Bothnia or to Narvik on Norway's west coast. Consisting of 50 wagons, up to 12 heavily laden trains run each day to Narvik and five to Lulea.*

▶ *This view of Stockholm Central station in 2002 shows, on the left, an SL (Storstockholms Lokaltrafiks – Tåg) locomotive-hauled suburban train and on the right an SJ (Statens Järnvägar) high-speed X2000 train. Introduced in 1990, a total of 43 sets of the latter Class X2 electric multiple units were fitted with tilting trailer cars for high-speed services on Swedish main lines. A few of these sets have been modified for services to Norway and Denmark.*

SWITZERLAND

The first steam railway in Switzerland, between Baden and Zurich, opened in 1847. Major rail tunnels through the Alps, such as the Gotthard (opened in 1882) and the Simplon (opened in 1906) have enabled the through-running of trains between other European countries and Italy. Today, Switzerland's railways are operated by numerous companies, of which Schweizerische Bundesbahnen (SBB) is the largest with a standard gauge all-electrified network of 3,011km/1,867 miles. Many other companies, of which Rhätische Bahn (RhB) is probably the most well known, operate metre-gauge/3ft 3⅜in electric railways in the more remote and mountainous regions of the country.

▲ *The privately owned RhB (Rhätische Bahn) operates 142km/88 miles of electrified metre-gauge/3ft 3⅜in lines in southeast Switzerland, including the separate Berninabahn and one route which crosses the Italian border to Tirano. The company operates several classes of electric locomotives, of which the Class Ge 4/4 I Bo-Bo, dating from 1947, is the oldest and the powerful Class Ge4/4 III Bo-Bo, introduced in 1993, is the newest. One of the latter class is seen in a garish livery promoting 'Riri the waterproof zipper' in April 2003.*

▶ *Originally opened in 1911 as part of the Furka-Oberalp-Bahn, the Dampfbahn Furka-Oberalp or Furka Heritage Railway is a privately owned steam-hauled rack-and-pinion railway that operates during the summer months between Realp and Oberwald in southern Switzerland. This section of mountain railway was closed in 1981 when the 5.5km/3.5-mile Furka Tunnel was opened through the Furka Pass. Reopened by railway preservationists in 2000, the Furka Heritage Railway operates steam locomotives such as No. 1 Furkahorn, here seen pounding uphill near Gletsch with a train from Realp in August 2005.*

▶ *A typical winter scene in Switzerland as a Rhätische Bahn train heads for the busy rail junction of Landquart in 2000. From Landquart, electric trains operate to the renowned ski resorts of Klosters and Davos, and to Chur for connection with the famous 'Glacier Express'. The narrow gauge RhB network contains 84 tunnels of which the longest at 19km/12 miles is the Vereina Tunnel between Klosters and Scuol.*

▼ *Opened in 1892, the BRB (Brienz-Rothorn-Bahn) is an 800mm/2ft 7.5in gauge steam-hauled rack-and-pinion mountain railway which climbs from the town of Brienz to a station close to the summit of the Brienzer Rothorn mountain, 2,244m/7,360ft above sea level. The line has gradients as steep as 25% (1 in 4) and passes through five tunnels on its 2.8km/1.7-mile route. Here, Class H2/3 No. 7, built in 1933, waits in the midway passing loop at Planalp station in May 1992.*

▲ Dubbed the slowest express in the world, the 'Glacier Express' takes nearly 8 hours to travel from Zermatt in southern Switzerland to St Moritz in the southeast of the country. Operated jointly by MGB (Matterhorn-Gotthard-Bahn) and the RhB (Rhätische Bahn) the metre-gauge/3ft 3⅜in line passes through some of the most dramatic mountain scenery in Europe, reaching an altitude of 2,033m/6,668ft at the Oberalp Pass. The steepest sections of line are operated by rack-and-pinion with motive power being provided by electric locomotives such as this MGB Class HGe4/4-II rack-and-adhesion locomotive seen hauling the 'Glacier Express' near Grengiols in August 1996.

◀ Equally owned by FS (Ferrovie dello Stato) of Italy and SBB (Schweizerische Bundesbahnen) of Switzerland, CIS (Cisalpino AG) operates tilting trains from cities in northern Italy to Geneva, Berne, Basel and Zurich in Switzerland. Introduced in 1996, a Cisalpino Class ETR.470 electric multiple unit is seen here at Bellinzona in southern Switzerland in June 2001.

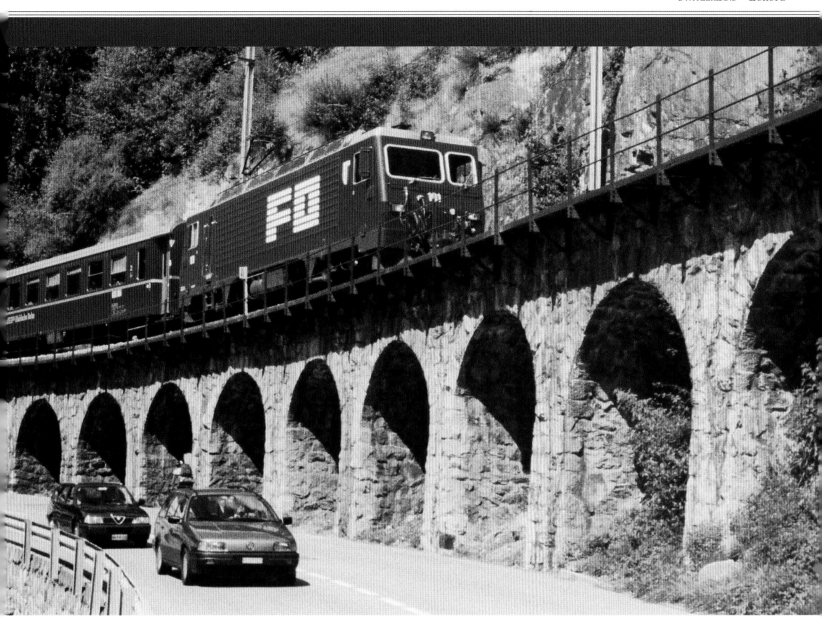

▶ Opened in 1893, the Wengernalpbahn (WAB) rack-and-pinion railway (the longest in Switzerland) connects the Alpine town of Wengen to Lauterbrunnen. Reaching an altitude of 2,061m/6,760ft at Kleine Scheiddegg, this scenic mountain railway is owned by JB (Jungfraubahn), which also operates a rack railway to the summit of the Jungfraujoch, at 3,454m/11,330ft above sea level the highest station in Europe. Introduced in 1988, this Class BDhe4/8 electric multiple unit is seen at Wengen station in March 1989.

UKRAINE

Railways in this former Soviet republic are now operated by UZ (UkrZaliznyza) and run on tracks using the old Russian 'broad' gauge of 1,524mm/5ft. UZ operates a large network of railways including 22,300km/13,826 miles of broad gauge lines, of which 9,169km/5,685 miles are electrified. Although gradually being replaced by more modern types, many former Soviet diesel and electric locomotives, with their distinctive 'kitsch' styling, can still be seen in operation.

▲ *An early Soviet-style 1960s-built Bo-Bo diesel switcher heads up a passenger train at Lviv station in July 2007. Located close to the Polish border in the far west of Ukraine, Lviv is one of the largest cities in the country. Due to its strategic location and industrial importance, the city is a major railway centre with international connections to Slovakia and Hungary. Lviv's imposing railway station was built in art nouveau style in 1903.*

▶ *Introduced in 1962, this Class ER2 electric multiple unit, seen at Mukacheve in July 2007, is a wonderful example of surviving 1960s Soviet railway styling. Mukacheve is a small historic city in southwest Ukraine, which until 1944 had a very large Jewish population.*

UK

In 1812, the Middleton Railway, a private industrial line in Leeds, became the first steam-hauled railway in the world. The first public steam railway in the world was the Stockton & Darlington which opened in 1825. What was known as 'Railway Mania' soon followed and 2,420km/1,500 miles had been built by 1840. Apart from Brunel's unique broad gauge of 2,140mm/7ft 0¼in and the Irish standard gauge of 1,600mm/5ft 3in, the standard rail gauge in the rest of Britain had been fixed at 1,435mm/4ft 8½in by 1846 – soon nearly every other country in Western Europe and North America were to follow suit. Following extensive closures after the Second World War, Britain's standard gauge rail network currently stands at 31,640km/19,660 miles, of which 13,120km/8,152 miles is electrified.

▲ In 1961, a former Great Western Railway County Class 4-6-0 heads an eastbound train past Parsons Tunnel signal box on the Dawlish sea wall in South Devon – one of the most scenic routes in the UK. Numbered 1000 to 1029 and designed by Frederick Hawksworth, a total of 30 of this class of locomotive were built at Swindon Works between 1945 and 1947. Although all members of this class were withdrawn from service and scrapped between 1962 and 1964, a replica of No. 1014 County of Glamorgan is currently being built at the Didcot Railway Centre in Oxfordshire.

▶ A Virgin Class 57/3 diesel hauls a Holyhead to London Euston Pendolino train along the North Wales coastal section of the West Coast Main Line at Colwyn Bay in 2004. Nicknamed 'Thunderbird', a total of 16 of the Class 57/3 locomotives were built to haul the electric Pendolino trains along this scenic non-electrified route and to act as standby locomotives for rescuing failed electric trains on other parts of the Virgin rail system. With a top speed of 225kph/140mph, a total of 53 nine-car sets of the tilting Class 390 Pendolino electric multiple units were built by Fiat Ferroviaria for Virgin Trains for use on the West Coast Main Line.

▲ The former LMS Princess Coronation Class 4-6-2 No. 46229, 'Duchess of Hamilton' catches the last rays of the setting sun while leaving Garsdale over Dandry Mire viaduct with a northbound Cumbrian Mountain Express on 29 October 1983. Passing through the Pennine Hills, the Settle to Carlisle line is one of the most scenic railways in the north of England and is a popular, although testing, route for steam-hauled special trains. Built in 1938 and originally fitted with a streamlined casing, 'Duchess of Hamilton' is one of three locomotives of this class to have been preserved and is part of the National Railway Museum Collection. A refit has supplied a streamlined casing similar to the one it lost in 1948.

◄ In its final year of steam haulage, a former Great Western Railway 'Castle' Class 4-6-0 heads the down 'Cornishman' at Bristol Temple Meads in 1962. Introduced by the Western Region of British Railways in 1952, this named train ran for ten years between Wolverhampton Low Level and Penzance with a detachable portion for Torquay and Kingswear. The train, with its brown-and-cream Mark 1 coaches, was usually hauled on the northern section between Wolverhampton and Bristol via Stratford-upon-Avon and Cheltenham by an immaculately clean Castle from the Stafford Road shed.

▶ Streamlined Coronation Class 4-6-2 No.6222 'Queen Mary' speeds through Hest Bank on the West Coast Main Line with the down 'Coronation Scot Express' from London Euston to Glasgow in 1937. Designed by William Stanier for the London Midland & Scottish Railway, a total of 38 of these powerful locomotives were built, of which 24 were streamlined. One member of this class, No. 6220 'Coronation' achieved what was then a British rail-speed record of 183.5km/h (114mph) just south of Crewe on 27 June 1937. The streamlined casing of these locomotives was removed after the Second World War to ease maintenance.

▶ *Class K1 2-6-0 No. 62012 and Class B1 4-6-0 No. 61243 double head a special working from Fort William across Crianlarich viaduct on 5 October 2002. Designed by Arthur Peppercorn, the last Chief Mechanical Engineer of the London & North Eastern Railway, the Class K1 were introduced in 1949 to work trains on the heavily graded and scenic Glasgow to Fort William and Mallaig line in the West Highlands of Scotland. Today, the 'Jacobite' steam train runs regular passenger services on the Fort William to Mallaig section of this line.*

▼ *Former LMS Royal Scot Class 4-6-0 No. 46162, 'Queen's Westminster Rifleman' stands ready to depart from London St Pancras station with the 11.45 Sunday express to Bradford on 12 March 1961. Designed by William Stanier, the Royal Scots were a rebuild of Henry Fowler's LMS locomotives, originally introduced in 1927, with a taper boiler, new cylinders and double chimneys. St Pancras Station, opened in 1868 as the London terminus of the Midland Railway, was designed by the engineer William Henry Barlow.*

YUGOSLAVIA

The first steam railway in former Yugoslavia, built as part of a railway line from Vienna to Trieste (then part of the Austrian Empire), opened in 1844. Yugoslav State Railways (JZ) was formed in 1945 after the independence of that country. Consequently, JZ inherited a collection of truncated main lines, locomotives and rolling stock from Austria, Hungary and Italy. Yugoslav State Railways ceased to exist as an integrated rail network on the breakup of Yugoslavia during the early 1990s.

▲ *Steam locomotives were used until well into the 1970s on Yugoslavia's railway network. Here, a Yugoslav State Railways Class 06 2-8-2 trundles across the River Drava at Maribor in 1972 with a local passenger train of four-wheel coaches. Maribor is now the second largest city in the new state of Slovenia. However, probably the most successful type steam locomotive ever built in Hungary was the MAV Class 424 4-8-0 which was reclassified as Class 11 in Yugoslavia. Nicknamed 'Buffalo', the first Class 424 was built in 1924 and by 1958, when construction ended, over 500 examples had been delivered for work not only in Hungary but also to neighbouring countries such as Yugoslavia and further afield in the Soviet Union and North Korea.*

▶ *On its formation in 1945, Yugoslav State Railways (JZ) inherited many Hungarian-built steam locomotives including the Class 22 2-6-2 introduced in 1909. Here the last example of this class lies out of use at Varazdin in modern-day Croatia after withdrawal from service.*

AFRICA

ALGERIA

The first steam railway in Algeria – then a French colony – opened in 1862 between Algiers and Blida. By 1946 there were 5,014km/3,109 miles of railways in the country, mainly in the north, of which much of this was narrow gauge. Since independence of the country in 1976, the railways of Algeria have been state-owned and operated by the Societé Nationale des Transports Ferrovaires (SNTF). Today, SNTF operates 2,888km/1,795 miles of standard gauge track, of which 2,893km/1,794 miles is electrified, and 1,085km/673 miles of narrow gauge (1,055mm/3ft 5½in)

▲ A busy scene at Relizane station as an SNTF express, hauled by a modern diesel-electric locomotive, arrives at the station in 1990. Located on the Oran to Algiers main line, Relizane is a French-style city in the fertile northwest of Algeria.

▶ Clearly showing its French origins, an SNTF 6CE electric locomotive heads for the coast near Drea at the head of a phosphate train in 1990.

BOTSWANA

The first railway, built by the Bechuanaland Railway Company, came to Botswana in 1897 as part of the major rail trunk route from Cape Town to the Victoria Falls. Soon after opening, the railway came under the control of the national railway owned by the South and North Rhodesia. On the creation of the Republic of Zimbabwe in 1980 the railways in Botswana came under the control of the National Railways of Zimbabwe (NRZ). The final twist in this tale of ownership came in 1987 when the Botswana Government bought the railways inside the country from NRZ and created Botswana Railways (BR). Today, BR operates 888km/550 miles of narrow gauge in the southeast of the country, connecting the border with Zimbabwe near Francistown to the South African border, southwest of Gabarone.

▲ Hauled by diesel-electric locomotive No. BD340, an intermodal freight train passes through Lobatse in southeast Botswana in 2000. Passenger services on Botswana's railways consist of one daily train each way between Francistown and the capital, Gaborone, and one overnight sleeper train each way between Francistown and Lobatse.

▶ The opening of the Beitbridge to Bulawayo Railway in 1999 bypassed the railways of Botswana and brought about a major drop in traffic on Botswana Railways (BR). Here, diesel-electric locomotive BD-111 refuels at Gaborone in 2000. A total of 12 of these locomotives were built for BR by Krupp of Essen, Germany in 1981.

ERITREA

The single narrow gauge (950mm/3ft 1⅖in) railway of the former Italian colony of Eritrea took 45 years to build. Starting at the Red Sea port of Massawa in 1887, the heavily engineered line climbed through the mountains to the capital, Asmara, where it arrived in 1911. With gradual extensions to Keren, Agat and Agorcat, the final terminus of Bascia was reached in 1932. The railway fell into disrepair during the Ethiopian civil war of the 1970s but has been rebuilt as far as Asmara since Eritrean independence in 1993.

▲ *Four of these 442 Series 0-4-4-0 compound Mallet locomotives were built by the Italian company of Ansaldo of Genova in 1938. All are still in existence on the Eritrean Railway and are used on tourist trains. Here a member of this class is seen on a works train near Digdigda in 1998.*

▶ *Built by Breda of Milan between 1927 and 1937, six of these little 202 Series of 0-4-0 tanks still survive on the Eritrean Railway. Here, one of this class is seen under restoration in the workshops at Asmara during the rejuvenation of the railway from Massawa to Asmara in 1998.*

▶ *Seen in the sheds at Asmara in 1998, this delightful diesel railcar is now used for tourist trains on the Eritrean Railway. Built by Fiat before the Second World War, three of these art deco-style 'Littorina' railcars still survive. Eritrean Railway also owns a few old diesel locomotives which are being restored to haul freight trains.*

▼ *Completed in 1911, the heavily engineered line up through the mountains from Massawa on the Red Sea coast to the capital, Asmara, involved the building of 65 bridges and 30 tunnels. Here a viaduct on this mountainous section awaits the relaying of track in 1998.*

GHANA

Built to a narrow gauge of 1,067mm/3ft 6in, the first railways in Ghana – then the British colony of Gold Coast – were built by the British at the end of the 19th century. As there were no harbour facilities all building materials, track, locomotives and rolling stock were manoeuvred onto dry land at Sekondi by lighters. The 304km/188 miles Eastern Railway opened in 1923 to convey mineral and cocoa to the new harbour at Takoradi. Following independence in 1957, the Ghana Railway Corporation took over the running of the 935km/580 miles of network. There are now plans in hand to rebuild the existing near-derelict and rundown railways, construct new standard gauge lines and extend the network further inland.

▲ Contrast in diesel designs at the Ghana Railway Corporation's Location Works on the branch line from Kojokrom to Sekondi in 1985.

▶ A narrow gauge industrial diesel with its train of side-tipping wagons.

◀ Built in Germany by Orenstein & Koppel, a brace of diminutive 0-6-0 industrial tank locomotives at the end of their working life at the Nsuta opencast manganese mine in June 1985. The mine, along with the largest gold mine in Ghana, is located near the railway junction town of Tarkwa in southwest Ghana.

▼ Steam traction on Ghana's railways ended in the mid-1980s and, apart from some industrial narrow gauge locomotives preserved at Nsuta manganese mine, nearly all of the withdrawn locomotives have now been scrapped. Built by Vulcan Foundry of Newton-le-Willows in Lancashire and fitted with a Giesl oblong ejector, this 4-8-2 of Ghana Railways, seen here in May 1985, ends its days beneath the coaling plant at Accra.

▲ Opened in 1907, the Ashanti gold mine is located at Obuasi, 200km/
124 miles northwest of the Ghanaian capital, Accra. The 15 mine shafts, some
more than 1.6km/1-mile below ground, are linked by an electric railway – here
seen in the photograph – with eight-car trains of side-tipping wagons hauled
British-built Clayton locomotives.

◄ Industrial steam locomotives once worked at the large opencast manganese
mine at Nsuta Wassa in southwest Ghana. Seen here at the mine in 1985,
this derelict 0-6-0 tank locomotive, built by W. G. Bagnall of Stafford, lies
in peaceful decline.

▲ By the mid-1980s the railways of Ghana were in a semi-derelict state and steam haulage had ceased altogether. Here, photographed at Kumasi locomotive shed in 1985, 4-8-2 No. 277 Dagomba makes a sad sight as it waits for the inevitable end. Built by Vulcan Foundry of Newton-le-Willows in Lancashire and fitted with one of Dr Giesl's oblong ejectors, one of these fine locomotives escaped the cutter's torch and was last seen in operation as a stationary boiler at a sawmill in Kumasi.

▶ Withdrawn Vulcan Foundry steam locomotives make an incongruous sight as they rub shoulders with the colourful daily market in the sidings at Accra station in May 1985. The current dereliction of Kumasi Station in Accra will hopefully end in the near future with the planned rebuilding and extension of Ghana's rundown Eastern Railway.

KENYA

After the First World War, the railways of the former British colonies of Uganda, Kenya and Tanganyika (now Tanzania) were jointly operated by East African Railways (EAR). The EAR was disbanded in 1977 and, until 2006, the railways of Kenya were operated by Kenya Railways Corporation. Since 2006, the Rift Valley Railways Consortium has taken operational control of both Kenyan and Ugandan railways. Built to the narrow gauge of 1m (3ft 3⅜in), the current network of railway lines in Kenya totals 2,778km/1,722 miles with the main route from Mombasa to Nairobi continuing through to land-locked Uganda. The railway was famous for operating massive 4-8-4+4-8-4 articulated steam locomotives (the most powerful metre-gauge locomotives in the world), first introduced in 1939, that were built by Beyer-Garratt of Manchester.

▲ *Nearing the end of its working life, an East African Railways Mountain Class 4-8-2+2-8-4 Beyer-Garratt departs from Voi with a freight train on the main line from Mombasa to Nairobi in 1973.*

▶ *The penultimate member of its class, No. 5933, this East African Railways metre gauge Class 59 'Mountain' 4-8-2+2-8-4 Beyer-Garratt is seen hauling a long freight train on the Mombassa to Nairobi mainline in the early 1970s. Beyer Peacock of Manchester built a total of 34 of these massive narrow gauge articulated locomotives in the 1950s for working the 534km/332-mile line from Mombassa on the Indian Ocean to the Kenyan capital of Nairobi. Two of these fine locomotives, No. 5918 'Mount Gelai' (in working order) and No. 5930 'Mount Shengena' are currently preserved in the Nairobi Railway Museum.*

MADAGASCAR

There are two separate metre-gauge/3ft 3⅜in railway systems on the island of Madagascar. The most southerly is the 163km/101 mile-long Fianarantsoa Cote Est (FCE) which links the highland city of Fianarantsoa with the east coast port of Manakara. Built by the French colonists between 1926 and 1936, this heavily engineered and steeply graded line was closed in 2000 following severe cyclone damage. The line has since been rebuilt and is now back in operation. To the north, the network of lines from the capital, Antananarivo, including the important link to the east-coast port of Toamasina (completed by Chinese workers in 1913) have been operated by Madarail since 2003.

▲ *Passengers halt for a lunch break at Ambatolampy on the line from Antananarivo to Antsirabe in 1992. The quaint railcar, built by De Dietrich of Niederbronn in France, dates from the 1950s.*

▶ *Seen here at Antananarivo 1992, this railbus was built by the French tyre company Michelin in the 1930s. Only four of these delightful vehicles survive in the world, including one that currently operates short tourist trips from Fianarantsoa on the FCE.*

MOROCCO

The first railways in the former French colony of Morocco were built for military reasons in the early 20th century with the majority of lines laid to the narrow 600mm/2ft gauge. Since then many of these lines have closed but others have been relaid to the standard gauge of 1,435mm/4ft 8½in and are now electrified. The current standard gauge system of 1,907km/1,182 miles, of which 1,003km/622 miles is electrified, has been operated by the state-owned ONCFM (Office Nationale des Chemins de Fer du Maroc) since 1963. Several high-speed lines are currently under construction and a rail tunnel under the Straits of Gibralter, linking Morocco with Spain, is now in its planning stage.

▲ An ONCFM train, hauled by a Co-Co electric locomotive crosses the impressive viaduct at Oued Yquem on the Rabat to Casablanca main line.

▶ Hauled by a Class DH 370 Co-Co diesel, a Fez to Oujda express enters the passing loop at Bab Merzoalla in 1990.

NAMIBIA

The first public railway in the former German colony of Namibia, then known as South West Africa, opened between the capital, Windhoek, and the west coast port of Swakopmund in 1902. During the period from the First World War to 1990, when the country was administered by South Africa, its railways were operated by South African Railways (SAR). After Namibia's independence in 1990, its railways came under the control of TransNamib who currently operate services on 2,382km/1,477 miles of narrow gauge track (1,067mm/ 3ft 6in). A new railway is currently being built northwards to link the system with Angola's railways.

▲ *Hauled by two General Electric Class U20C diesels, a double-headed goods train carrying jet fuel from the port of Swakopmund to the capital, Windhoek, passes Osona in December 1999.*

▶ *Painted in the bright yellow and blue colours of NaRail (the new name for TransNamib), a former South African Railway U20C diesel electric locomotive passes through Sobabir in February 2000.*

SOUTH AFRICA

The first steam railway in South Africa, between Cape Town and Wellington, opened in 1860. Laid to a gauge of 1,067mm/3ft 6in, the majority of South Africa's rail network was completed by the time the country became a British dominion in 1910. From this date all of South Africa's railways came under the control of the South African Railways & Harbours until 1990, when it was reorganised as Transnet. With links to the rail systems of Namibia, Botswana, Zimbabwe and Mozambique, over 50 per cent of the current network of about 20,000km/12,400 miles is electrified.

▲ Until the early 1980s, South Africa's railways were one of the last strongholds of mainline steam haulage in the world. Here, double-headed by a Class 25 4-8-4 and Class 15CA No. 2817, the latter built by American Locomotive Company in 1926, an iron ore train departs from Senekal on the Marquard to Wolwehoek line in June 1975.

▶ The Outeniqua Choo-Tjoe is a steam-hauled heritage line that runs along the Garden Route from George, location of the Dias & Outeniqua Transport Museum, to Knysna on the shores of the Indian Ocean. The scenic 52km/32 mile railway was opened on 17 October 1928 and since 1992 has operated as South Africa's only steam-operated heritage line. Although trains are scheduled for steam traction, they are occasionally hauled by diesels during periods of drought and an increased risk of veld fires.

▲ A pair of SAR Class 15AR 4-8-2s, Nos. 2015 and 1787 – both built by North British Locomotive Company – double-head an East London to Cape Town train in July 1975.

◄ Previously known as Spoornet, Transnet Freight Rail is South Africa's main line rail operator and the largest rail freight haulier in Africa. Here, in Spoornet livery, electric locomotive E1691 is seen in the busy freight yard at Belfast on the electrified line between Pretoria and Maputo in Mozambique in March 2002.

▶ *A Class 7E electric locomotive and its massive coal train crosses the White Umfolozi River in the Umfolozi Game Reserve in northeast Natal. This line links Richard's Bay – the largest harbour in South Africa and the largest single export coal terminal in the world – with coalfields in Broodsnyersplaas via the town of Vryheid.*

▶ Still steam-hauled in July 1976, this Cape Town to Port Elizabeth train is seen departing from Oudtshoorn, a town in Klein Karoo in the far south of the country. By 1985 this line had been dieselised and the only steam left operating in the area was on the George to Knysna branch to the south.

▼ This SAR 4-8-2 makes a fine sight at the head of a northbound express at Karee, north of Bloemfontein, in the 1970s. By March 1985, services on the mainline from Bloemfontein northwards to Kroonstad had been taken over by diesels. Only the short branch from Theunissen to Winburg remained steam-hauled.

SUDAN

Laid to a gauge of 1,067mm/3ft 6in, the first railways in the Sudan were built by the British military south from Wadi Haifa in the north of the country in the 1870s. Later operated by Sudan Railways, the network, including a plantation railway with a narrower gauge of 610mm/2ft, had grown to a length of 5,311km/3,293 miles by 1961 when the line to Wau in the southwest of the country was completed. The busiest section has always been that from the capital, Khartoum, to the Red Sea port of Port Sudan. There are currently plans to extend the rail network to Uganda, Kenya and the Central African Republic.

▲ Built by the North British Locomotive Company of Glasgow, these two Class 500 4-8-2s – one off the rails and one on the rails – were photographed here between Rabak and Kenana in 1983. Steam traction on Sudan Railways lingered on until 1990.

▶ Diesel power was introduced to Sudan Railways in the late 1950s and ten mainline diesels – looking not unlike their famous Deltics – were supplied by English Electric to Sudan Railways in the early 1970s. Here, one of their earlier units with its classic American-inspired styling could still be found, albeit in a rundown condition, in 1983. These early diesels were replaced by more modern General Electric Class U15 A-1-A and Class UM22C C-C diesel locomotives in the 1970s.

▲ Lit by the setting sun, this North British Class 500 4-8-2 is seen hauling a mixed train between Rabak and Kenana in central Sudan in 1983. Formed in 1903, the North British Locomotive Company of Glasgow became the largest locomotive building company in Europe. Until the 1950s the company was a major supplier of powerful steam locomotives to railways around the world, including Australia, New Zealand, South Africa and Sudan.

◀ Too much regulator and not enough sand! A Sudan Railways 4-8-2 slips vigorously on greasy rails in 1983.

▶ A steam railcar, built by Clayton of Lincoln in the 1920s, lies abandoned at the end of the branch line from Sennar Junction at Ad-Damazin in 1983. Specialising in the construction of rolling stock and steam railcars, the Clayton Carriage & Wagon Company of Lincoln ceased trading in the early 1930s.

▲ *Also built by the suppliers of steam locomotives to the British Empire – the North British – this dilapidated Sudan Railways 4-6-2 No. 240 languishes at Old Sennar Junction in 1982. Sennar Junction is an important railway crossroads on Sudan Railways with lines radiating out to Khartoum in the north, Kassala and Port Sudan in the east, Ad-Damazin in the south and Nyala and Wau in the far west.*

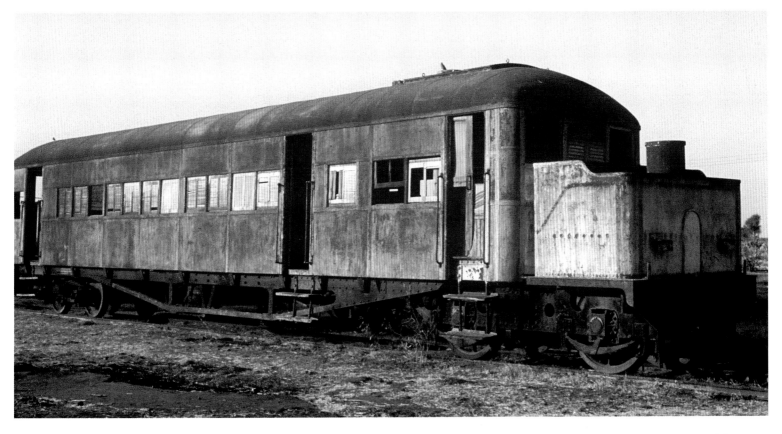

TANZANIA

There are two separate rail systems in Tanzania – the state-controlled Tanzania Railways Corporation (TRC) operates 2,600km/1,612 miles of metre-gauge/3ft 3⅜in that was once part of the extensive East African Railways Corporation. The TRC provides rail transport from Dar es Salaam on the coast of the Indian Ocean to Kigoma on the shores of Lake Tanganyika, to Arusha in the northwest and on a long branch to Mwanza on the southern shores of Lake Victoria. With a total length of 1,860km/1,152 miles, the Tazara Railway was built by the Chinese in the 1970s to a gauge of 1,067mm/3ft 6in and links Dar es Salaam with the landlocked railways of Zambia.

▲ *A light axle load former East African Railways 2-8-2 built by the Vulcan Foundry in Newton-le-Willows, Lancashire, heads a freight from Tabora along the lonely branch line to Mpanda in western Tanzania in 1983.*

▶ *Formerly owned by the East African Railways, this Tanzania Railways Class 60 Governor Beyer-Garratt 4-8-2+2-8-4 replenishes its water supply as it heads for Voi in Kenya with an overnight freight from Moshi in Tanzania.*

ZIMBABWE

The railways of Zimbabwe were originally an important link in the uncompleted continuous railway line intended to link Cape Town in South Africa with Cairo in Egypt. Known as Rhodesian Railways until 1980, Zimbabwe's rail system is now operated by the National Railways of Zimbabwe (NRZ). With a gauge of 1,067mm/3ft 6in and a network of around 3,000km/1,860 miles, NRZ has important links with neighbouring countries such as South Africa, Zambia, Mozambique and Botswana. A new railway line from Beitbridge on the South African border to Bulawayo was opened in 1999.

▲ An engineer of Rhodesia Railways oversees as a 20th-Class Beyer-Garratt 4-8-2+2-8-4, takes on water at Matetsi with a freight train from Bulawayo bound for Victoria Falls and Zambia in 1973.

▶ A 20th-Class 4-8-2+2-8-4 Beyer-Garratt departs from the Wankie coalfields in the northwest of the country heavily laden with coal for Bulawayo and Salisbury (Harare) in 1973.

◄ Rhodesia Railways 14th-Class Beyer-Garratt 2-6-2+2-6-2, takes refreshment at Balla Balla on its way from West Nicholson on the branch line to Bulawayo in 1973. Built in large numbers by Beyer-Peacock of Manchester, many of these powerful articulated locomotives once operated on the narrow gauge railways of southern Africa. In recent years, steam power in the shape of these monster locomotives has survived longer in Zimbabwe due to ample local coal supplies and shortages of diesel fuel caused by the current economic and political unrest.

ASIA

CHINA

The first steam railway in China, from Shanghai to Woosung, opened in 1876. Due to a combination of civil wars and war with Japan, the Chinese rail network was slow to expand in the early 20th century. However, since the Second World War many new lines have been built in China, including the line from Guangzhou to Urumqi, the Jitong Railway in Inner Mongolia and the Qingzang railway to Tibet. Now with a network length of 76,600km/47,492 miles of standard gauge (1,435mm/4ft 8½in) track, the state-owned railways of China – known as China Railways and the third largest network in the world – are primarily the responsibility of the Ministry of Railways and its 18 railway bureaus or railway group companies.

▲ *Only a year before the end of main line steam in China in 2005, two Class QJ 2-10-2s head an eastbound freight over the curved viaduct at Simingyi on the Jitong Railway, Inner Mongolia.*

▶ *Banked in the rear by a Class QJ 2-10-2, a China Railways Class JS 2-8-2 climbs away from Nancha with a passenger train in the 1990s. More than 800 of the Class JS locomotives were built by the Dalian Locomotive and Rolling Stock Works between the late 1950s and early 1960s.*

▲ *A China Railways diesel-electric tops the summit at Wang Gang with a southbound train from Harbin in 1985. Due to the abundance of coal and labour, the majority of China's railways remained steam-hauled until the 1980s. Introduced in 1959, the first home-grown diesel-electric locomotives were the Dongfeng (DF) class of which thousands of various types have been produced by locomotive works at Sifang, Ziyang and Dalian.*

◄ *China Railways Class SL6 4-6-2 passes Saddle Mountain on the approach to Anshan on the Dalian to Shenyang main line in 1985. Around 800 of the Class SL6 locomotives were built by Sifang Locomotive and Rolling Stock in the 1950s.*

▶ A typical winter railway scene in northern China, during the final days of steam, is seen here. Featured are two of the famous Class QJ locomotives at the head of a long freight train on the Jitong Railway. Developed from the German Kriegslok 2-10-0s of the Second World War and the subsequent Russian L-Class 2-10-0, more than 4,700 of the Class QJ 2-10-2 locomotives were built at the Datong Locomotive Works in China between 1956 and 1988. They were not only the last main line steam locomotives built in the world but many also remained in regular service on the Jitong Railway until December 2005. Several examples of this class have since been preserved and kept in working order.

◄ Steam's swan song! Undoubtedly one of the most remote and exciting railways in the world, the Jitong Railway in Inner Mongolia was also the last to see regular steam haulage, and in the early 21st century became a magnet for railway photographers around the world. The thrill and excitement of live steam is summed up in this photograph of a pair of Class QJs blasting their way through the icy wastes with a long freight train on the Jitong in 2003.

▼ A Swiss look-alike, this is one of China's many Crocodile electric locomotives, which proliferated in mining environments throughout the country. These 1,500 V DC locomotives were built in Eastern Europe and China. The original Swiss Crocodiles were built between 1919 and 1927 for Swiss Federal Railways and were used to haul freight trains through the Gotthard Tunnel.

▲ Opened in 2004, the Tianjin Binhai Mass Transit is a light rail system that links Tianjin, an industrial city in northeast China, to the Tianjin Economic-Technological Development Area. Here seen in 2005, the majority of the route is elevated and runs parallel to the Jintang Exressway. With a total length of 53km/33 miles, the line is the longest rapid transit system in China.

▶ Steam finale – another double-headed QJ operation on the Jitong Railway, Inner Mongolia, in the final year of steam operation.

INDIA

The first steam railway in India, a short section of the then-new Great Indian Peninsular Railway from Bombay, opened in 1854. Much broader than in most other countries, a 'standard' gauge of 1,676mm/5ft 6in was chosen for many of the lines. Many narrow gauge railways were also built to various gauges – 1,000mm/ 3ft 3in, 762mm/2ft 6in and 610mm/2ft. The rail network was initially slow to expand but by the time of independence in 1947 it had reached a total of 65,000km/40,300 miles. Now operated by Indian Railways, the current network of 63,140km/39,147 miles is the fourth largest in the world and carries more than 5 billion passengers each year.

▲ Now designated a World Heritage Site by UNESCO, the Darjeeling Himalayan Railway (here seen in 1975) opened in 1881 from Siliguri to Darjeeling in West Bengal. Using a succession of loops, the 610mm/2ft gauge railway climbs 2,100m/6,888ft over a distance of 86km/53 miles. The railway is still mainly steam-hauled using Class B 0-4-0 saddle tanks, some of which date from 1892. A total of 34 of these powerful but diminutive locomotives were built by Sharp Stewart of Manchester, North British Locomotive Company of Glasgow and the Baldwin Locomotive Works of Philadelphia between 1889 and 1925.

▶ An Indian Railways standard 'broad gauge' Class XD 2-8-2 at work on the South Central Railway during the 1970s. The last example was delivered in the 1940s, after a total of 200 Class X Dominion locomotives were built and were widely used for freight duties. None have survived.

▲ Women hack clay from the earth to supply Ledo Brickworks in Upper Assam. Operating on a gauge of 610mm/2ft, this private narrow gauge railway is located in the North Eastern Coalfields and was still steam hauled until recent years. Two diminutive 0-4-0 saddle tanks locomotives – 'Namdang', built in 1894 by W G Bagnall of Stafford, and 'David', built in 1924 – operate on a short stretch of line hauling sand to the brickworks.

▲ Shortly before the end of steam in India, an Indian Railways metre-gauge (3ft 3⅜in) Class YG 2-8-2 heads the afternoon passenger train from Morvi to Wankaner in 1999. The first examples of this class were built in Germany and by the Baldwin Locomotive Works of Philadelphia. Others were later built in India by Chittaranjan Locomotive Works and Telco with the last being delivered nearly forty years ago in 1972.

▲ A timeless scene as women fill their urns with water, with the connivance of the fireman, from the tender of an Indian Railways metre-gauge Class 2-8-2 on the Morvi to Wankaner line in 1999. Located in Gujarat state, close to the Pakistan border in northwest India, the railway served an area known for its agricultural produce and cotton processing.

▲ Another idyllic rural scene as the last survivor of South Eastern Railway's Class HSM 2-8-0 heads along the Fort Gloster branch on the outskirts of Calcutta in 1979. Located on the Ganges delta in West Bengal and close to the border with Bangladesh the Fort Gloster branch saw some of the last regular 'broad gauge' steam trains in India. Fitted with a larger superheated boiler, the Class HSM locomotives were a development of the Class H 2-8-0s originally introduced by the Bengal Nagpur Railway in 1903.

▲ *One of the last examples of an Indian Railways Class XE 2-8-2 is seen here at work on menial duties at Chunar Cement Works in the late 1980s. The Class 'X Eagle' 'broad gauge' locomotives were the most powerful freight locomotive in India. Vulcan Foundry of Newton-le-Willows, Lancashire built 51 examples of this class, after the Second World War. Class XE No. 3634 has been preserved and restored to working condition.*

◄ *The riot of primary colours reflect typical Hindu art and brighten up this little Indian Railways locomotive seen at Lucknow in 1976. Fitted with Caprotti valve gear, the Class XT 0-4-2 tank locomotives were built in the 1940s in the Ajmer workshops for use on light passenger duties. Serving the metre-gauge (3ft 3⅜in) Rajputana-Malwa Railway, in 1895 Ajmer Workshop had the distinction of building the first steam locomotive in India.*

▲ A proud line-up of Indian Railways 'broad gauge' steam locomotives at Howlah Depot, Calcutta, in 1976. Left to right: WP Class Pacific; Class XC Pacific; British-built inside cylinder 0-6-0. In all 755 of the distinctive Class WP 4-6-2s were built between 1947 and 1967 for use on express passenger trains. The initial batch was produced by the Baldwin Locomotive Works of Philadelphia in the USA, but later examples were home-produced at the Chittaranjan Locomotive Works of Mihijam, West Bengal. Several examples are preserved in working order. Many Class XC 4-6-2s were built by the Vulcan Foundry in the late 1920s for various Indian railways, including the East Indian Railway, the Bombay Baroda & Central Indian Railway and the Great Indian Peninsular Railway.

▶ Seen at Asanol Depot in Bengal in 1976, Indian Railways Class WP Pacific 4-6-2 No. 7247 has been beautifully turned out and decorated in readiness for the regional locomotive beauty contest held annually in Delhi.

स्वयंवर

7247 WP

INDONESIA

The first steam railway in what is now Indonesia, between Semarang and Tanggung in Java, opened in 1867. It was built to the standard gauge of 1,435mm/4ft 8½in and was owned by the Nederlandsch-Indische Spoorweg (Netherlands East Indies Railway Company). Due to the high cost of construction other railways were built to a narrower gauge of 1,067mm/3ft 6in or, in the case of plantation lines, 600mm/1ft 11⅝in. Railway building continued in both Java and Sumatra but the Depression of the 1930s, the Japanese occupation during the Second World War and the war for independence all took its toll and many lines were closed. Today, around 6,000km/3,720 miles of mixed narrow gauge tracks are operated by the state-owned PT Kereta Api.

▲ *Steam continued to be used on Indonesia's railways until the 1980s. Here, an Indonesia Railways Class C12 two cylinder compound 2-6-0 tank locomotive is seen at work on the island of Java in 1974. Diesel locomotives were first introduced in 1953 when 27 Co-2-Co locomotives were ordered from the US. This was followed by a much larger order of around 250 locomotives, delivered between 1957 and 1967, which displaced steam power from most main lines.*

▶ *Many narrow gauge railway lines in Indonesia were built to serve sugar plantations and factories, tobacco and rubber plantations, and forestry. Here, a German Orenstein & Koppel tank locomotive is at work at the Meritjan Sugar Mill in Kediri on Java in 1974. The job of the man sitting on the front of the locomotive was to spray sand on the tracks ahead of the engine to improve adhesion on slippery rails.*

▶ Here working at the Trangkil Sugar Mill on Java in 1989, this tiny 0-4-2 saddle tank became the last industrial steam locomotive to be exported from Britain when it was delivered from the Hunslet Engine Company of Leeds in 1971. Coincidentally, in the late 19th century, the first steam locomotive built for export by Hunslet was also for a railway in Java, India.

▼ With its spark-arresting chimney, this diminutive Orenstein & Koppel 0-6-0 tank locomotive is seen at work on a 600mm/1ft 11⅝in gauge stone-carrying railway in northern Sumatra in 1974. Founded in Berlin, Germany, in 1876, Orenstein & Koppel was a major supplier of narrow gauge steam locomotives around the world. Their last steam locomotive was built in 1969 and since then many of these little workhorses have been preserved in working order.

JAPAN

British-built and financed, the first steam railway in Japan, from Shimbashi to Yokohama, opened in 1872. It was built to a narrow gauge of 1,067mm/3ft 6in and, strangely, apart from the new Shinkansen lines, this still persists as the standard gauge in Japan today. Japan's rail network was severely damaged during the Second World War but, as the country's economy improved, the late 1950s and early 1960s saw a rapid turnaround of its railways' fortunes. The world's first modern dedicated high-speed line, the Tokyo Shinkansen, opened in 1964 and since then the Shinkansen network has expanded with the building of new routes and major tunnels and bridges linking Japan's main islands. The last steam locomotives were retired in 1975.

▲ In contrast to Japan's older railways, the new high-speed Shinkansen routes were built to a gauge of 1,435mm/4ft 8½in. The 300 Series Shinkansen trains seen here in 2005 were introduced in 1992 and operate at speeds of up to 270km/h (167mph) on the Tokaido Shinkansen and the Sanyo Shinkansen routes. Built of aluminium, a total of 69 sets were built, each set comprising 16 carriages.

▶ The Series 100 Shinkansen, here seen with an up Hikari service entering Hiroshima station in 1997, were built between 1984 and 1991 for the Tokaido Shinkansen and Sanyo Shinkansen routes. Now replaced by the 300 Series and new 700 Series on the Hikari services on these routes, the Series 100 are now relegated to slower 'Kodama' services on the Sanyo Shinkansen.

▲ The classic Bullet Train – a Series 100 Shinkensen speeds past Mount Fuji in 1994. The first Shinkansen high-speed trains were operated by Series 0 sets, which were introduced on the Tokaido Shinkansen route in 1964, have now retired from service. An instant success with the travelling public and an enormous public relations coup for Japan's railways, the Series 0 sets of up to 16 carriages initially ran at speeds of up 210km/h (130mph).

◀ An unusual duty for 1960s-built electric freight locomotive No. EF66 44 seen here at the head of a 'Sakura' passenger service at Tokyo Central in 1998. Apart from a few other narrow gauge lines, Japan's principal rail network is made up of 20,264km/12,564 miles of narrow 1,067mm/3ft 6in gauge (over half electrified) and 3,204km/1,986 miles of 1,435mm/4ft 8½in standard gauge (all electrified) routes.

▶ A futuristic line-up of Shinkansen trains at Tokyo Central station in 1998.
Designed in Germany and introduced in 1997, the Series 500 Shinkansen of
JR West (on the left) is the fastest and most expensive of the Shinkansen trains to
be built to date. Capable of speeds of up to 320km/h (198mph), only nine sets
of 16 carriages were built and these are used on the premium 'Nozomi' super
express services. The Series 400 trains, as seen on the right, are known as
'mini Shinkansen' because they operate on the narrow clearances of existing
1,067mm/3ft 6in gauge lines that have been converted to Shinkansen
standards. Introduced in 1992, they operate on the Tohoku Shinkansen
and the Yamagata Shinkansen routes.

MALAYSIA & SINGAPORE

Built to serve local tin mines, the first steam railway in Malaysia, between Port Weld and Taiping, opened in 1885. The first railway on the island of Singapore opened in 1903 and the railway causeway linking Singapore with Malaysia was opened in 1923. Laid to a narrow gauge of 1,000mm/3ft 3⅜in, the main rail network of Malaysia today extends to 1,669km/1,035 miles and includes two main lines: one along the west coast links Singapore with Thailand and the other, an east coast line, links Tumpat and Gemas. Plans to build a standard gauge high-speed line between Kuala Lumpur and Singapore are currently on hold.

▲ The island of Singapore is linked to the Malaysian mainland by a causeway and through railway services on the metre-gauge (3ft 3⅜in) main line operate between Singapore and the Malaysian capital, Kuala Lumpur. The heavily populated island of Singapore also has a modern Mass Rapid Transit system (MRT), which opened in 1987. The current network of 109km/68 miles consists of three main lines with a total of 67 stations. Here, an MRT train is seen near Ang Mo Kio station on the North South line in 2004.

▶ The 134km/83 mile-long metre-gauge (3ft 3⅜in) Sabah State Railway is the only rail system on the island of Borneo. The line was opened to serve tobacco plantations in 1896 and, despite being severely damaged during the Second World War, currently operates a service between the inland town of Tenom and the west coast port of Tanjung Aru. Here, a diesel-hauled passenger train is seen at the line's western terminus of Tanjung Aru in 1998.

PAKISTAN

The first steam railway in what is now Pakistan, between Karachi and Kotri, was opened in 1861. With strong British influence, the main railways of what was then northwest India were built to a 'broad' gauge of 1,676mm/5ft 6in with many secondary lines laid to a narrow gauge of 1,000mm/3ft 3⅜in. At the time of independence in 1947, Pakistan inherited 8,122km/5,036 route miles from the former North Western Railway of India and, in 1961, was renamed Pakistan Railways. Many of the narrow gauge lines are being converted to broad gauge but plans were announced in 2006 to convert the country's railways to the standard gauge of 1,435mm/4ft 8½in to make them compatible with those of neighbouring China.

▲ The broad gauge railways of the Punjab were a magnet for broad gauge steam popular with enthusiasts well into the 1980s. Here, British-built inside cylinder 0-6-0 No. 2505 puts on a fiery show at the local depot in the mid-1970s.

▶ The crew of this beautifully turned-out British-built inside cylinder 0-6-0 pose for the camera at the head of a passenger train on Pakistan's broad gauge in 1984. The lower quadrant semaphore signal is yet another example of the strong British influences then found on Pakistan's railways.

▶ *Steam lingered on in Pakistan well into the 1980s. Here, a Pakistan Railways metre-gauge (3ft 3⅜in) 4-6-2 locomotive sidles up to the water column on the Mirpur Khas network in the southeast of the country. The metre-gauge railway to Khokhrapar has recently been converted to broad gauge. After 40 years of railway separation between India and Pakistan, a new rail link has also been opened through Mirpur Khas linking Karachi (Pakistan) with Jodhpur (India).*

PHILIPPINES

Built to the narrow gauge of 1,067mm/3ft 6in, the first steam railway in the Philippines, then a Spanish colony, opened in 1892 between Manila and Dagupan on the island of Luzon. There are currently two separate rail systems on Luzon: Northrail is a 266km/165-mile line from Manila to San Fernando but has been closed since the 1980s; Southrail is a 479km/297-mile line from Manila to Legazpi City which is still operating but in a rundown state. Until recently the last bastion of steam in the Philippines, the once extensive network of industrial narrow gauge lines serving sugar cane plantations and the forestry industry have almost completely disappeared.

▲ With an almost Wild West appearance, the Insular Lumber Company's 0-6-6-0 four cylinder compound Mallet heads a rake of tree trunks over the viaduct at Maarslud in 1974. Built in 1924, this powerful locomotive worked the lumber lines on Negros Island until 1975 and is currently preserved in non-working condition at Sangay.

▶ Occasionally steam-hauled for visitors, the Hawaiian Philippine Sugar Mill rail network on the island of Negros is still in operation. Here, 'Dragon No. 6' 0-6-0 crosses a girder bridge in 1974.

SAUDI ARABIA

The first railway in Saudi Arabia was the southern section of the Hejaz Railway which opened in 1908 to transport pilgrims from Damascus in Syria to Medina in Saudi Arabia. The line closed during the First World War. Currently, the Saudi Railway Organisation operates a modern network of 1,018km/631 miles with other routes such as the Saudi Landbridge in the planning stage.

▲ *Built by the Ottoman Empire to a gauge of 1,050mm/3ft 5⅓in, the Hejaz Railway was an immediate success with pilgrims to Mecca when it opened in 1908. Used by the Turks as a military railway during the First World War, the Hejaz soon came under attack from Lawrence of Arabia and his Arab allies. Many sections of the line were destroyed and the line closed in 1915. However, it is still possible to travel from Damascus in Syria to Amman in Jordan along the original northern part of the railway. Seen here, the ghostly remains of a repair train lies in the sands at Buwayr in northern Saudi Arabia following blitz and subsequent destruction by Lawrence more than 90 years ago.*

▶ *More remnants of the Hejaz Railway still lie in the sands at Hadiyah in Saudi Arabia nearly a century after Lawrence of Arabia's second attack on the railway during the First World War. To date, there have been several unsuccessful attempts to reopen this historic railway.*

SYRIA

Syria was the starting point for the famous Hejaz Railway, which was built by the Turks to link Damascus in Syria with Medina in Saudi Arabia. Opened in 1908, the Hejaz had a short life conveying pilgrims on their way to Mecca. During the First World War it was used by the Turks to convey troops and came under attack from Lawrence of Arabia and his Arab allies. The line closed in 1915 and has not reopened although the northern section from Damascus to Amman in Jordan is still operational. The other strategic railway in Syria, via Aleppo, was a section of the controversial Berlin to Baghdad Railway. Sections of this line remain in use today.

▲ *Built by the German locomotive company of Borsig in 1914, this Syrian Railways oil-burning 2-8-0 was seen in action at the important junction station of Dera'a on the border with Jordan in the mid-1970s. Steam haulage on this northern section of the Hejaz Railway continued into the 21st century.*

▶ *This Syrian Railways 2-8-0, built by the German locomotive company of Hartmann, was seen abandoned at Cadem Works in Damascus in the mid-1970s. The Cadem Works was the main workshop for the Hejaz Railway and was still being used to repair steam locomotives in the early 21st century.*

▲ Headed by an SLM 2-6-0 tank locomotive, a Friday excursion train heads away through the mountains above Damascus bound for the cool relief of the hill country. Here seen near Serghaya near the Lebanese border in the mid-1970s, the line from Damascus Baramke to Beirut was a branch of the Hejaz Railway and built to a gauge of 1,050mm/3ft 5⅓in.

◄ Built by Hartmann in 1907, Syrian Railways 2-8-0 No. 91 traverses the Syrian section of the Hejaz Railway with the daily mixed train from Dera'a to Damascus. These powerful narrow gauge locomotives were the mainstay of steam motive power on this northern section of the railway during the latter part of the 20th century.

TAIWAN

The first steam railway on the island of Taiwan opened in 1891. The main line network was laid to a gauge of 1,067mm/3ft 6in with many other industrial lines, serving forestry, mining and sugar cane plantations, laid to a gauge of 762mm/2ft 6in. More recently a new high-speed line and city metros have been built to the standard gauge of 1,435mm/4ft 8in. Today, Taiwan's rail network of 1,496km/928 miles is mainly operated by the Taiwan Railway Administration. Most of the once-vast network of industrial lines, in particular those operated in the south east by Taiwan Sugar, have more-or-less completely disappeared.

▲ *Mainline steam traction clung on in Taiwan until the mid-1970s. Here, a Taiwan Government Railways Class CT262 4-6-2 belches smoke at Chiayi depot in 1974. These powerful narrow gauge locomotives were built to the design of Japan's National Railway C57 Class C57 Pacifics. Located in south-central Taiwan, Chiayi is also famous for the Alishan Forest Railway, which operates a tourist train through forests to the popular mountain resort of Alishan.*

▶ *A line-up of Taiwan Railways motive power at Hsinchu depot in 1974. Today, the city of Hsinchu in northwest Taiwan is an important centre for high-tech companies and is served by TRA trains between the capital, Taipei, and Kaohsiung.*

TURKEY

Built by a British company, the first steam railway in Turkey, between Izmir and Aydin, opened in 1856. After this, other countries, in particular Germany and France, were also given licenses by the then Ottoman Empire to build railways to serve industries and seaports. Following the end of the Ottoman Empire in 1923, rail building in the new Turkish Republic gathered pace and 3,578km/2,218 miles were added to the network by 1950. Although electrification of some main lines started in 1977, the Turkish Republic State Railways (TCDD) has seen a significant drop in traffic in recent years. New high-speed railways, including that from Istanbul to Ankara, are currently under construction. The railways of the Middle East and Europe will also be physically linked for the first time in 2012 when the Marmaray rail tunnel beneath the Bosphorus is opened.

▲ *One of the celebrated TCDD 2-10-0 Skyliners, built by the Vulcan Iron Works in the US after the Second World War, is seen here at the head of a passenger train travelling from Irmak to Zonguldak on the Black Sea coast in 1986. The area around Zonguldak is an important centre for coal mining and coal trains continued to be steam hauled into the 1980s.*

▶ *Built in Sweden for Tubize-Nohab, 53 of the Class G8 2-8-0 heavy freight locomotives were supplied to the TCDD in 1932. Here, the ultimate member of this class, No. 45062, makes a fine sight as it heads a southbound freight at Masya in the mountains of northern Turkey in 1977. The last members of this class were only withdrawn from services in 1990.*

▶ After the Second World War, the TCDD ordered a total of 88 powerful 2-10-0 locomotives from the Vulcan Iron Works in the US. Delivered between 1947 and 1949 they became known as Skyliners and, because of their large boiler and firebox, were fitted with mechanical stokers. Here a Skyliner darkens the sky as it heads a loaded coal train from the Black Sea collieries in the mid-1970s.

▼ While Turkey remained neutral during the Second World War, its railway system was supplied with steam locomotives from the US, UK and Germany. A total of 53 of the United States Army Transportation Corps S200 Class 2-8-2 locomotives found their way to Turkey during and just after the war. Many continued in use until the latter part of the 20th century. Here, one of these powerful locomotives heads away from Irmak with a light freight for Cankiri in the mid-1970s. One example of this class, No. 46244, has been preserved and is on display at Camlik Railway Museum near Ephesus.

AUSTRALASIA

AUSTRALIA

The first steam railway in Australia, the Melbourne and Hobson's Bay Railway from Melbourne to Port Melbourne, opened in 1854. Many of Australia's early railways were built to a gauge of 1,600mm/ 5ft 3in (the same as in Ireland) but by 1901, when the six separate colonies became a federation, five different gauges were in use across the continent. This lack of standardisation caused severe problems and was a stumbling block to railway modernisation until a few years ago. Today, Australia's rail network of 33,819km/20,968 miles includes the Alice Springs to Darwin section of the Adelaide to Darwin line, which has taken 130 years to complete.

▲ *National Rail locomotive No. NR50 at the head of 'The Ghan' leaving Goulburn, New South Wales in January 2000. 'The Ghan' is a luxury train that operates between Adelaide and Darwin via Alice Springs and takes 48 hours to complete the 2,979km/1,847-mile journey. The train gets its name from an abbreviation of the Afghan camel trains that once operated this route in the 19th century.*

▶ *The road ahead for New South Wales Railway Class 79 4-4-0 locomotive No. 1243 on the approach to Ashwell with a train from McAlister in May 1969. The Class 79 was introduced in 1877 for mainline express passenger services and some have been preserved, including No. 1243.*

◄ Introduced in 1957, 100 of the New South Wales Class 44 Co-Co diesel locomotives were built by A E Goodwin and were fitted with ALCO engines. Most of these workhorses were withdrawn from service in the 1990s but six have since been preserved. Here, No. 4481 is seen in the freight yard at Goulburn, New South Wales in 1993.

▼ A line-up of New South Wales Railways preserved standard gauge locomotives at Goulbourn in 1973 includes 4-4-0 No. 176, Class Z17 4-4-0 No. 1709 built by Vulcan Foundry of Newton-le-Willows in Lancashire in 1887 and the famous streamlined Class 38 4-6-2 built by Clyde Engineering in 1943.

▼ The Pichi Richi Railway is a heritage railway that operates between Port Augusta and Quorn in the Flinders Ranges in South Australia. Opened in 1879 and built to a gauge of 1,067mm/3ft 6in, this line was once the starting point for the Afghan Express trains to Alice Springs. On conversion of that route to standard gauge the Pichi Richi Railway was closed to traffic in 1957. A well-preserved 4-6-2 No.W933 returning to Quorn in South Australia with a Pichi Richi Railway Preservation Society train in 1994.

▲ Introduced in 1951, a total of 47 of these US-style GM Class Co-Co diesel locomotives were built by Clyde Engineering for Commonwealth Railways. This company operated services on standard gauge track 1,435mm/4ft 8½in on the former Trans-Australia Railway and the Central Australia Railway. It was merged as part of the Australian National Railways Commission in 1975. Here, resplendent in its former livery, the premier member of this class, GM1, was seen at Spencer Junction Yard at Port Augusta, South Australia, in 1997.

▶ Some claim the New South Wales Railways Class P6 4-6-0s of 1892 were the technical prototype for the Highland Railway Jones Goods 4-6-0 locomotives. Whatever the story, the P6 (which became the Class C32 from 1924) was one of Australia's most successful passenger designs with 191 being built by Beyer Peacock of Manchester in the UK by 1914. Four of these locomotives have since been preserved including No. 3214, here seen in its full glory as it powers towards Oolong in 1977.

NEW ZEALAND

Built to a gauge of 1,600mm/5ft 3in, the Lyttelton & Christchurch Railway became the first steam railway in New Zealand when the first section from Christchurch to Ferrymead opened in 1863. By 1877 the narrower gauge of 1,067mm/3ft 6in had been adopted as the 'standard' gauge throughout the country. Following wholesale closures of lines on both North and South Islands in the 1960s and 1970s and more recent drastic curtailment of many passenger services, the present network of 3,898km/2,417 miles is a shadow of its former self with the majority of lines carrying freight only.

▲ *Tranz Rail diesel shunter No.2341 waits ready for action at Wellington in 2003.*

▶ *Located on New Zealand's South Island, The 'Kingston Flyer' is a steam-operated heritage train that operates for 14km/9 miles along part of the former branch line from Gore and Invercargill to Kingston. Here, trains once connected with a steamer service across Lake Wakatipu to Queenstown. Today, a train of seven wooden vintage carriages dating from 1898 are hauled by former New Zealand Railways Class AB 4-6-2 locomotives, including No. 795, which was a former Royal Train locomotive. Here, sister engine No. 778, built in 1925, nears Fairlight with the 'Kingston Flyer' in 1991.*

▲ Apart from services between Picton, Blenheim, Christchurch and Greymouth all surviving passenger services on South Island were withdrawn in 2002. However freight tonnages have significantly increased since the New Zealand rail network was re-nationalised in 2003. Here, a typical container train headed by DFT Co-Co diesel No. 7145 passes through Kaikoura on South Island with a southbound freight in 1999. The DFT Class of Co-Co diesel-electric locomotives are a rebuild of the former New Zealand Railways DF Class of which a total of 30 were built by General Motors in Canada between 1979 and 1981.

◀ Introduced in 1988, the 'TranzCoastal' is a long-distance passenger train that runs between Picton and Christchurch on New Zealand's South Island. Here, the 'TranzCoastal' passes Kekerengu, south of Blenheim in 2004.

▶ *Attached to a generator van, Class DX No. 5258 passes Makotuku on New Zealand's North Island with the daily 'Bay Express' from Wellington to Napier in 1991. Passenger services on North Island to Tauranga, Rotorua and Napier ceased in 2001 and famous trains such as the 'Geyserland Express' and the 'Bay Express' passed into history. The only passenger services still operating in North Island are between Wellington and Auckland and Wellington and Masterton. A total of 49 locomotives of the DX Class Co-Co diesel-electric locomotives were built by General Electric in USA for New Zealand Railways between 1972 and 1975.*

NORTH AMERICA

CANADA

The first steam railway in Canada, between Laprairie near Montréal and St Johns, opened in 1836. Railway expansion from east to west was slow and the first route, built for the Canadian Pacific Railway, was not completed until 1885. There then followed 30 years of unprecedented expansion of the rail system – the 17,100km/10,602 miles built by 1886 had tripled by 1914. Despite wholesale closures of uneconomic branch lines in the 1960s, the present standard gauge network totals 49,922km/30,952 miles and handles significant amounts of freight traffic, most of it handled by the two major privately owned companies, Canadian National and Canadian Pacific. Passenger traffic is provided by VIA Rail.

▲ Formed in 1978, VIA Rail operates all long-distance passenger trains in Canada over a network of 14,000km/8,680 miles stretching from Halifax in the east to Vancouver in the west and from Windsor in the south to Churchill in the north. Here, a VIA Rail express leaves Montréal headed by one of the latest General Electric Class P42DC 'Genesis' B-B diesel-electric locomotives in 2005.

▶ Built in large numbers for railroads in the United States, Canada and Mexico, the General Motors EMD SD40-2 C-C diesel-electric locomotive, seen here in tandem crossing a bridge at North Adams, Massachusetts, has been one of the workhorses of the Canadian Pacific Railway fleet since it was introduced in the 1970s and 1980s. By 1986, nearly 4,000 of these 3,000hp locomotives had been built, of which 484 had gone to CPR.

▶ To haul freight trains on its massive network Canadian Pacific Railway operates nearly 1,700 diesel-electric locomotives. Built by the Montréal Locomotive Works in the 1960s, Class RS-18 No. 1820 was photographed at St Martins Junction, Quebec in January 1993. The last two units of this class were retired in 1998.

▼ Formed in 1919, Canadian National Railways is the longest railway system in North America and controls more than 50,000km/31,000 miles of track in Canada and the US. Dieselisation of the system was complete by 1960 and CNR currently operate around 1,500 locomotives including this yard set comprising a GP9V plus SLU6 seen in Montréal, Quebec in 2005.

CUBA

The first steam railway in Cuba, then a Spanish colony, opened between Havana and Bejucal in 1837. The standard gauge network, expanded in the early 20th century by the Canadian railroad investor William van Horne, currently extends to 4,226km/2,620 miles. Following the Cuban revolution in 1959 the majority of the country's railways were nationalised and are now operated by Ferrocarrriles de Cuba (FdeC). Much-needed equipment has been supplied by China and Iran but some steam locomotives can still be found working on sugar cane plantation lines.

▲ *Much of Cuba's railway system is run down and in need of modernisation. Many of the diesel-electric locomotives in operation, such as this example seen in the yard at España in 2003, are of 1950s vintage and are Soviet copies of US locos.*

▶ *Steam clung onto life in poverty-stricken Cuba much later than in the rest of North America. Here a Baldwin Locomotive Works 2-6-0 of 1920s vintage passes a classic American-style wooden signal box on stilts at Robles in 1988. In addition to the FdeC railway system there are thousands of miles of sugar cane plantation railways on Cuba, some of which still operate vintage steam locomotives.*

USA

The first steam railway in the US, the Baltimore & Ohio Railroad, began operating in 1830. By the end of that year there were only 23 miles/37km of completed standard gauge railways in the whole of the country, but growth was rapid and by 1890 there were 129,488 miles/208,851km. Today, while much-reduced passenger services are operated by Amtrak, US railroads convey vast quantities of freight over a network of 226,097km/140,180 route miles.

▲ The Southern Pacific Railroad's 'Coast Daylight' express between Los Angeles and San Francisco made its inaugural run behind a Class GS2 4-8-4 in 1937. Making the 756km/469-mile trip in daylight hours, the train continued to be steam-hauled until 1955 when it was dieselised. Here a magnificent Class GS2 shows the typical smoke plume of an oil burner while hauling the 'Coast Daylight'. Six of these streamlined locomotives were built by the Lima Locomotive Works but none have survived. Amtrak may soon resurrect the 'Coast Daylight', which last ran in 1971.

▶ The National Railroad Passenger Corporation, or Amtrak, is a US government-owned corporation that was formed in 1971 to provide long-distance passenger train services throughout the country. It operates services over a 33,810km/21,000-mile network mainly on track owned by other railroads and links around 500 destinations in 46 US states and in Canada. Here, the 'Empire Builder' express from Chicago to Seattle and Portland is seen at Grizzly Park in Montana in 1994. Passenger traffic on Amtrak is now seeing an upturn following years of declining passenger numbers.

▲ Known as a Mikado, or Mike for short, the 2-8-2 wheel arrangement became one of the most popular type of steam locomotives in the US. First introduced before the First World War, more than 14,000 were built and they remained the most common freight locomotive on many railroads until the 1950s. Here a typical Mikado, No. 40, is seen at work on the Connecticut Valley Railroad in 1996.

◄ US railroads carry billions of tons of freight each year. Here, a quartet of Burlington Northern & Santa Fe Railway diesels power a container stack train up the ascent near Alroy in Cajun Pass, California in 2000. One of the largest railroad networks in North America, the BN&SF was formed in 1996 by the merger of the Atchison, Topeka & Santa Fe railway and the Burlington Northern Railroad. Unlike European railways with their restricted loading gauge, intermodal double-stacked freight trains are now common on US railroads because of their generous loading gauge.

▶ The 914mm/3ft gauge Cumbres & Toltec Scenic Railroad was originally opened as part of the Denver & Rio Grande Railroad's network of lines built to serve the silver mines in the San Juan Mountains in southwest Colorado. Opened in 1880, the 103km/64-mile steam-hauled line was saved from closure in 1970 and now operates steam-hauled passenger trains between Chama and Osier and from Antonito to Osier. Here, Class K-37 2-8-2 No. 497 is seen at Windy Pass on the Cumbres & Toltec in 1997. No. 497 was originally built as a standard gauge locomotive by the Baldwin Locomotive Works in 1908 but was rebuilt to the 914m/3ft gauge in the railroad's Burnham Shops in 1930.

◀ Built by Lima-Hamilton Corporation in 1948, Class J3 4-8-4 No. 614 became the last commercially built mainline steam locomotive to be assembled in the US. The loco had a short but successful life hauling express trains on the Chesapeake & Ohio Railroad between Richmond and Chicago until being displaced by diesels in 1952. After languishing for decades in a roundhouse and as a static exhibit, No. 614 was finally restored to her former glory in 1980 and since then has hauled special trains in the US at up to speeds of 129km/80mph. Seen here at Green Briar in 1981, No. 614 is a monster of a machine and a match for any diesel – 5m/16ft tall, 34m/112ft long, weighs 434 tons and develops around 5,000 horsepower.

▼ The 'Adirondack' is a long-distance passenger train operated by Amtrak between New York City and Montréal in Canada, a distance of 613km/381 miles. A high-speed rail link between the two cities is now planned as the current journey takes 10 hours at an average speed of 61.3km/38.1mph. Here, the 'Adirondack' is seen leaving Montréal headed by a General Electric Class P32ACDM diesel-electric locomotive in 2007.

SOUTH AMERICA

ARGENTINA

The first steam railway in Argentina, from Buenos Aires and Floresta, was opened in 1857. As no gauge for this line had been specified, locomotives built to a gauge of 1,676mm/5ft 6in, originally intended for use in India, were purchased for the line at the end of the Crimean War. Thus the Argentinian rail gauge was decided. Mainly financed and built by the British, the country's rail network had expanded to 47,000km/29,140 miles by 1920. The private rail companies were nationalised in 1948 and the network was then operated by Ferrocarriles Argentinos (FA) until the 1990s when it was privatised again. Today, Argentina's rundown railway network of 34,059km/21,117 miles operates on five different gauges. A high-speed railway is planned to link Buenos Aires with Rosario and Cordoba.

▲ The commuter lines around Buenos Aires were privatised in the 1990s. Here, a suburban electric multiple unit leaves Constitucion station in downtown Buenos Aires on the line to La Plata line in 2004.

▶ Saved from complete closure in 1992, the narrow gauge La Trochita in Patagonia is now operated as a heritage line. Seen here in 2005, a Baldwin-built 2-8-2 crosses the viaduct close to El Maiten on its journey to Esquel in the foothills of the Andes.

◄ The building of the narrow gauge railway known as La Trochita in Patagonia was severely curtailed by flood damage in 1931 and 1932. Aided by government funding and a workforce of 1,000 immigrant labourers much of the line was rebuilt with new bridges and a tunnel before it finally opened to Esquel on 25 May 1945. Here, a Baldwin-built Mikado is seen working a train to Esquel in 1990.

▼ Formed from various private railways including the British-owned Buenos Aires Great Southern Railway in 1948, the nationalised Ferrocarril General Roca (FCCR) operated the network of railways to the south and southwest of Buenos Aires. Here, looking very much like an Irish narrow gauge locomotive, an ancient 2-6-0 tank built by one of the oldest locomotive builders in the world – Nasmyth Wilson of Patricroft, Manchester – is seen at work on this rundown broad gauge system in 1979.

BOLIVIA

The most important railway to be built in landlocked Bolivia was the extension of the 762mm/2ft 6in narrow gauge line from the Chilean Pacific Coast at Antofagasta, which was opened as far as Oruro in 1892. Climbing over the Andes at altitudes of 4,500m/14,760ft, this line was converted to metre gauge (3ft 3⅜in) in 1928 and operates today as the Ferrocarril de Antofagasta a Bolivia (FCAB). Although no passenger trains operate today, the railway's primary traffic has always been carrying minerals, mainly copper ore.

▲ Maintenance work takes place on an ex-Ferrocarril de Antofagasta a Bolivia (FCAB) metre-gauge (3ft 3⅜in) 4-6-2, built by Henschel of Kassel, Germany, in 1914. Laid to serve nitrate and copper mines in the 1870s, this famous trans-Andean line is still operational and was steam-hauled until being phased out by diesels in the 1960s and 1970s.

▶ A former Argentine Railway standard gauge Urquiza Q Class 2-8-0, built by the North British Locomotive Company of Glasgow between 1913 and 1914. The locomotive was subsequently sold to Bolivia and is seen here undergoing overhaul in the works at Uyumi at the time of Che Guevara's assassination in 1967.

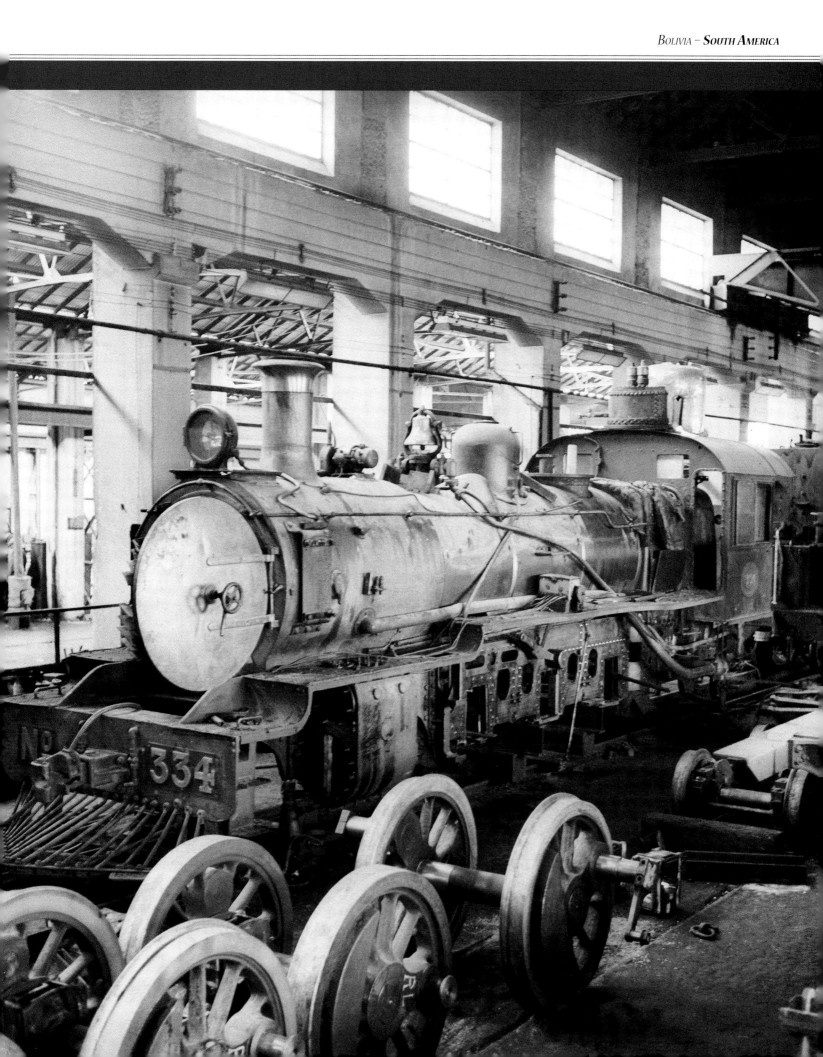

BRAZIL

Built to a gauge of 1,600mm/5ft 3in, the first steam railway in Brazil was the first section of the Dom Pedro II Railway in Rio de Janeiro in 1852. By 1975, the country's rail network had reached a length of 30,430km/ 18,867 miles, which included lines built to four different gauges. Since then several new heavy-duty freight lines have been built and there has been a modernisation programme of gauge conversion and electrification. Formed in 1957, the Rede Ferroviaria Federal, Sociedade Anonima (RFFSA) was the state-owned nation rail system until privatisation at the beginning of the 21st century. A high-speed railway link between Rio de Janeiro and Sao Paulo is in the planning stage.

▲ The last working steam locomotives in Brazil were to be found on short industrial lines. Here, a 0-4-0 vertical-boilered steam locomotive, built by Sentinel of Shrewsbury, works out its final days at a wagon works near Sao Paulo in 1979.

▶ An electric suburban train leaves Luz Station on the urban rail system operated by Companhia Paulista de Trens Metropolitanos (CPTM) around the city of Sao Paulo. Designed by the English architect, Henry Driver, this imposing station with its famous clock tower was built using material imported from England and completed in 1901 as the headquarters of the British-built and financed Sao Paulo Railway.

▲ A line-up of metre-gauge (3ft 3⅜in) diesels from the rail system of Brazil's mining giant, Companhia Vale do Rio Doce (CVRD). The CVRD is the world's biggest producer of iron ore and operates an extensive railway system linking its mining operations with ports on Brazil's Atlantic seaboard. The company, known as Vale, has invested heavily in new locomotives and freight cars, primarily for iron ore transportation. It currently operates more than 800 locomotives and over 35,000 freight cars.

▶ A blast from the past: this classic American switcher, or shunter, built by Baldwin Locomotive Works, US, in the 1890s, had been pensioned off to industrial service at an iron and steel works near Sao Paulo in 1979.

CHILE

The railways of Chile can be split into two very different sections: in the south, the 1,676mm/5ft 6in gauge lines were built by the famous American railway engineer Henry Meiggs in the 1860s; in the north, a network of metre-gauge (3ft 3⅜in) lines, including the Transandine rack and adhesion railway to Argentina, were built by brothers Juan and Mateo Clark but not completed until 1910. Other separate west–east narrow gauge lines, including the famous Ferrocarril de Antofagasta a Bolivia (FCAB), were built to tap enormous mineral deposits, especially copper and sodium nitrate. Today, the national railway of Chile, Empresa de los Ferrocarriles del Estado (EFE), operates services on a rundown network of 6,782km/4,205 miles of broad gauge and narrow gauge track.

▲ Adorned with the colourful company livery, a Type 9 diesel-electric locomotive heads a copper train on the FCAB metre-gauge (3ft 3⅜in) line to Antofagasta in northern Chile in 1999.

▶ There are very few steam locomotives in operation in Chile now. One of them, broad gauge 2-8-2 No. 714, built by ALCO in 1919, is based in Santiago to haul special charter trains. Here, No. 714, guarded by a set of ancient double-aspect semaphore signals, passes under more modern overhead wiring on Chile's rundown and overgrown system in 1990.

ECUADOR

The main railway in Ecuador, the Guayaquil & Quito railway was built to a gauge of 1,067mm/3ft 6in and it had taken 37 years to complete the zig-zag line by the time it opened in 1908. With a length of 450km/279 miles this mountainous line had gradients as steep as 1in 18 with a summit of 3,552m/11,651ft above sea level. Earthquakes and massive landslides have seriously curtailed through-services on this line.

▲ ▶ *Sadly, the Guayaquil & Quito Railway is currently in a very rundown state and through services are impossible since sections of the line have been seriously damaged by the earthquakes and floods. Here, seen at work in happier days, are 2-6-0 No. 14 (above), built by the Baldwin Locomotive Works of Philadelphia in 1901, and 2-6-0 No. 11 (right), also built by Baldwin in 1900.*

PARAGUAY

Built to a gauge of 1,676mm/5ft 6in, the first steam railway in Paraguay opened in 1859. Today, the country's rail system (since converted to 1,435mm/4ft 8½in gauge) has been reduced to a single line operating between the capital, Asuncion, and Encarnacion on the Argentine border, a distance of 376km/233 miles. The future of this railway, operated by Ferrocarriles del Paraguay S. A. (FE.PA.S.A), which was still regularly using steam locomotives into the 21st century, is very uncertain.

▲ Totally separate from the rest of Paraguay's railway system and located 674km/418 miles north of Asuncion on the Paraguyuan Chaco, the 150km/93-mile Puerto Casado Railway was a 762mm/2ft 6in gauge forestry railroad run by the Compania Carlos Casado. Here, 'Don Carlos', a 2-8-2 wood-burning well tank built by Manning Wardle of Leeds in 1916, is seen at work in 1980.

▶ Laurita, an 0-4-0 wood-burning well tank here seen on the Puerto Casado Railway in 1979, was built by Arthur Koppel in 1898. It was recently reported that the town of Puerto Casado and surrounding land had been purchased by followers of Sun Myung Moon, or 'Moonies', as they are known.

PERU

There are two distinctly different railways in Peru. The Ferrocarril Central Andino (Peruvian Central Railway) links the Pacific port of Callao with Huancayo and Cerro de Pasco. Built in the 1870s by the famous American railroad engineer, Henry Meiggs, the line reaches an altitude of 4,818m/15,803ft above sea level as it crosses the Andes at La Cima. Further south, the Ferrocarril del Sur (Peruvian Southern Railway) links the Pacific port of Matarani and the city of Arequipa with Cusco, Machu Picchu and the Quillabamba Valley. With a summit of 4,313m/14,147ft, a branch line from Cusco ends at Puno on the northern shore of Lake Titicaca.

▲ The standard gauge Ferrocarril del Sur (Peruvian Southern Railway) currently operates diesel-hauled tourist trains from Cusco to Puno on the northern shores of Lake Titicaca. In the past these trains were hauled by steam locomotives such as this 2-8-0 No.82, built by ALCO-Rogers in the US in 1907, seen here at Puno in the early 1960s.

▶ High up in the Andes, locomotive No. 107 heads a train on the 914mm/3ft gauge section of the Ferrocarril Central Andino (Peruvian Central Railway) between Huancayo and Huancavelica in May 1981. Formerly of the Trujillo Railway, Hunslet of Leeds built No.107 in 1936. Until the opening of the railway from China into Tibet, the FCCA was the highest in the world and its 490km/304-mile route includes 68 tunnels, 61 bridges and 9 switchbacks. Current operations concentrate on the haulage of bulk cargoes including minerals, fuels, cement and food products. The FCCA also operates a diesel-hauled bi-monthly tourist train between Lima and Huancayo and a steam charter train is also available.

INDEX

ACKNOWLEDGEMENTS

The Publishers would like to thank Julian Holland for his hard work, patience and perseverance throughout the creation of this book.

The Automobile Association wishes to thank the following photographers and organisations for their assistance in the preparation of this book.

All images provided by Milepost 92½ - railphotolibrary.com with the exception of:

35 AA/M Jourdan; 76–77 Great Southern Rail; 90–91 AA/C Sawyer; 115 AA/P Kenward; 202–203,215 David Cox; 204b,205,206–207, 211,212t Tom Greaves; 216b,221 Richard Pelham; 220b Chris Walker

Every effort has been made to trace the copyright holders, and we apologise in advance for any unintentional omissions or errors.
We would be pleased to apply any corrections in any following edition of this publication.

Full-page continent captions

EUROPE *Page 8–9:* With Ben Lui in the background, Class 37 diesel No. 37261 heads for Oban with the 'Royal Scotsman' train alongside the River Lochy on 4 June 1986. British Rail introduced the highly successful Class 37 diesels in 1960 and a total of 309 locomotives were built over the next five years by English Electric at their Vulcan Foundry in Newton-le-Willows, Lancashire, and by Robert Stephenson & Hawthorns of Darlington. A few examples of this popular workhorse still remain in service while many others have been preserved. Operating throughout the Highlands of Scotland, the 'Royal Scotsman' – one of the most luxurious trains in the world – is a plush cruise train operated by Orient-Express Hotels Ltd and is composed of five state carriages (cars), two dining carriages, one observation carriage and a crew carriage.

AFRICA *Page 90–91:* The Outeniqua Choo-Tjoe, here seen traversing the Kaaiman's River Bridge, is South Africa's only remaining scheduled steam train and operates along the Garden Route, part of which runs alongside the Indian Ocean.

ASIA *Page 130–131:* The late afternoon sun highlights a heavy eastbound freight, double-headed by two Class QJ 2-10-2 locomotives, passing Guangtai on the Jitong Railway in Inner Mongolia in 2004. With a length of 945km/585 miles, the Jitong Railway links Jining with Tongliao and was opened in 1995. Until diesels took over in December 2005, it became famous for being the last main line in the world to use steam power.

AUSTRALASIA *Page 176–177:* Closely watched by one of the natural inhabitants, the Great Southern Railway crosses the Australian outback between Sydney and Perth with the 'Indian Pacific' luxury train. This twice-weekly service only became possible in 1970 after the trans-continental line was converted to standard gauge. Before that, a change of train was necessary at Broken Hill where the different gauges met. The 'Indian Pacific' takes 65 hours to complete its 4,352km/2,698-mile journey across southern Australia and traverses the world's longest stretch of straight railway line (478km/296 miles) across the Nullarbor Desert.

NORTH AMERICA *Page 188–189:* An Amtrak train passes through Emigrant Gap, in the Sierra Nevada Mountains, California in 1998. Emigrant Gap, on the former Southern Pacific Railroad line between Reno in Nevada and Sacramento in California, is so named as it was an important crossing point of the Sierra Nevada Mountains for emigrants and their wagon trains heading west in the 1840s.

SOUTH AMERICA *Page 202–203:* Known as 'La Trochita' and made famous by Paul Theroux in his book 'The Old Patagonian Express', this Argentinean narrow gauge railway is an amazing survivor of steam; the line having faced complete closure in 1992. Opened between 1935 and 1945 in the foothills of the Andes in Patagonia, the 750mm/2ft 5½in gauge line runs for 402km/250 miles between Esquel and Ingeniero Jacobacci and is now operated as a heritage railway. Here a Class FA75B 2-8-2 locomotive, built by the Baldwin Locomotive Works of Philadelphia in 1922, and its train of vintage coaches wends its way through the Patagonian landscape between El Maiten and Norquinco with a special train to Carro Mesa in September 1990.